CANAL

Vol 3

STAFFORDSHIRE

by

JOHN N. MERRILL

Maps and Photographs by John N. Merrill

1989

i

a J.N.M. PUBLICATION

JNM PUBLICATIONS,
WINSTER,
MATLOCK,
DERBYSHIRE.
DE4 2DQ

Conceived, edited, typeset, designed, marketed and distributed by John N. Merrill.

© Text and routes — John N. Merrill 1989

© Maps and photographs — John N. Merrill 1989

First Published — January 1989

ISBN 0 907496 62 8

Meticulous research has been undertaken to ensure that this publication is highly accurate at the time of going to press. The publishers, however, cannot be held responsible for alterations, errors or omissions, but they would welcome notification of such for future editions.

Printed by — Amadeus Press Ltd., Huddersfield, West Yorkshire.

ABOUT JOHN N. MERRILL

John combines the characteristics and strength of a mountain climber with the stamina and athletic capabilities of a marathon runner. In this respect he is unique and has to his credit a whole string of remarkable long walks. He is without question the world's leading marathon walker.

Over the last fifteen years he has walked more than 100,000 miles and successfully completed ten walks of at least 1,000 miles or more.

His six major walks in Great Britain are —
Hebridean Journey .... 1,003 miles
Northern Isles Journey...913 miles
Irish Island Journey .... 1,578 miles
Parkland Journey .... 2,043 miles
Lands End to John o'Groats .... 1,608 miles
and in 1978 he became the first person (permanent Guinness Book of Records entry) to walk the entire coastline of Britain — 6,824 miles in ten months.

In Europe he has walked across Austria — 712 miles — hiked the Tour of Mont Blanc, completed High Level Routes in the Dolomites, and the GR20 route across Corsica in training! In 1982 he walked across Europe — 2,806 miles in 107 days — crossing seven countries, the Swiss and French Alps and the complete Pyrennean chain — the hardest and longest mountain walk in Europe, with more than 600,000 feet of ascent!

In America he used the the world's longest footpath — The Appalachian Trail -2,200 miles — as a training walk. He has walked from Mexico to Canada via the Pacific Crest Trail in record time — 118 days for 2,700 miles. In Canada he has walked the Rideau Trail.

During the summer of 1984, John set off from Virginia Beach on the Atlantic coast, and walked 4,226 miles without a rest day, across the width of America to Santa Cruz and San Francisco on the Pacific Ocean. His walk is unquestionably his greatest achievement, being, in modern history, the longest, hardest crossing of the USA in the shortest time — under six months (178 days). The direct distance is 2,800 miles.

Between major walks John is out training in his own area — the Peak District National Park. As well as walking in other parts of Britain and Europe he has been trekking in the Himalayas five times. He has created more than ten challenge walks which have been used to raise more than £250,000 for charity. From his own walks he raised over £80,000. He is author of more than ninety books, most of which he publishes himself. His book sales are in excess of 2 million.

CONTENTS

INTRODUCTION 1

JAMES BRINDLEY 2

TRENT & MERSEY CANAL 3

WALK 1 — WILLINGTON — 2½ miles (2 WALKS) 4

WALK 2 — STRETTON — 3 miles 6

WALK 3 — STRETTON — 2½ miles 8

WALK 4 — BURTON UPON TRENT — 4½ miles 10

WALK 5 — BRANSTON — 6 miles 12

WALK 6 — BARTON TURN — 5 miles 14

WALK 7 — ALREWAS — 6 miles 16

WALK 8 — FRADLEY JUNCTION — 5 miles 20

WALK 9 — HANDSACRE — 4½ miles 22

WALK 10 — HANDSACRE — 4 miles 24

WALK 11 — RUGELEY — 5½ miles 26

WALK 12 — RUGELEY — 3 miles 28

WALK 13 — LITTLE HAYWOOD — 4 miles 30

WALK 14 — SEVEN SPRINGS — 7 miles 32

WALK 15 — GREAT HAYWOOD — 5 miles 36

WALKS 16 & 17 — WESTON — 4 & 7 miles 38

WALK 18 — ASTON — 4 miles 42

WALK 19 — WESTON — 7 miles 44

WALK 20 — STONE — 5 miles 46

WALK 21 — MEAFORD — 7 miles 50

WALK 22 — BARLASTON — 3½ miles 52

WALK 23 — BARLASTON — 5 miles 54

WALK 24 — END TO END — 42 miles 56

COVENTRY CANAL 59

WALK 1 — HUDDLESFORD — 3 miles 60

WALK 2 & 3 — TAMWORTH — 4½ AND 8 miles 62

STAFFORDSHIRE & WORCESTERSHIRE CANAL 65

WALK 1 — TIXALL BRIDGE & TIXALL — 4 miles 66

WALK 2 — TIXALL BRIDGE & STAFFORD — 5 miles 68

WALK 3 — ACTON TRUSSELL — 4 miles 70

WALK 4 — HATHERTON JUNCTION — 3½ miles 72

WALK 5 — END TO END — 15 miles 74

ABOUT THE WALKS 76

CANAL FEATURES 77

CANAL MUSEUMS AND OTHERS OF RELATED INTEREST 78

CANAL SOCIETIES 80

SUGGESTED FURTHER READING 81

OTHER CANAL BOOKS BY JOHN N. MERRILL 82

OTHER BOOKS BY JOHN N. MERRILL 83

WALK RECORD CHART 85

CANAL BADGE ORDER FORM 86

EQUIPMENT NOTES 87

THE COUNTRY CODE 88

THE HIKERS CODE 89

SHADE HOUSE LOCK

SINAI PARK

TRENT & MERSEY CANAL, STONE

INTRODUCTION

For the last six months I have been walking the canals of Staffordshire and surrounding areas gradually piecing this book together. For me it has been an enjoyable time treading new ground and learning about areas that I had only motored through in the past. Like my other two canal books, my aim was simple — to explore each canal from end to end doing circular walks. Not just exploring the canal but its setting and surrounding villages to encompass more of the area. Many places came as a surprise, for I hadn't expected to see such peaceful scenery with so much historical content.

As in the other books in this series, I have had to shut my mind off to some areas simply because the book would become too big. As a result I have endeavoured to confine myself with the Trent & Mersey, Coventry and Staffordshire & Worcestershire Canals; thus starting and ending where volumes One and Two ended. This is the missing link! I have omitted the Shropshire Union Canal as I plan to deal with this in a future volume. Likewise the Birmingham Canals will be done in two volumes. So you can see, as one book closes the plans and scope for others does not decrease!

Here then is a stunning array of a variety of walks in Staffordshire, enabling you to explore and see at first hand the "motorway system of yesteryear". They have provided me with exercise and endless pleasure. I can only hope as you put your boots on and walk the area that you too are enthralled at what the area has to offer.

HAPPY WALKING!

John N. Merrill.

JOHN N. MERRILL.
Derbyshire. 1988

1

JAMES BRINDLEY — INN SIGN FROM
GAS STREET BASIN, BIRMINGHAM

JAMES BRINDLEY — 1716-1772

James Brindley, the greatest canal engineer of his time, was born at Tunstead, near Wormhill, Derbyshire. At Wormhill is a drinking trough to his memory. He was uneducated and could hardly read or write. From an early age he was fascinated by mechanical things. He saw a corn mill and sketched the parts to understand how it worked. At the age of 17 he went to work for a millwright, named Abraham Bennett, at Sutton near Macclesfield. He soon showed a natural talent for designing mechanical works using water. He earned himself a nickname — 'the schemer' — for his now apparent genius. On one occasion he worked at a mill on one of the Duke of Bridgewater's estates.

His skill soon reached the ears of the Duke, and so began one of the major partnerships in transportation. The Duke needed engineering advice, for he wanted to move coal from his mines on the Worsley estate to the port of Manchester. He had devised a canal but was stuck at making locks. Brindley suggested an aqueduct, which was thought unrealistic by the establishment. But the Duke could see it was a good sound idea, and it was built — 900 yards long and 17 feet high — carrying the canal over the River Irwell at Barton. The canal was opened in 1761 and became the wonder of the year. This immediately reduced the price of coal in Manchester from 17d(7p) a hundredweight to 3½d(1½p).

Whilst canals were already being built for short distances, Brindley's expertise launched the country into a fervour of activity, with the next 80 years being the canal's heyday — until the advent of railways. With the Duke he went on to construct 360 miles of canals. His next project was the Manchester — Liverpool Canal, 24 miles long. Brindley was poorly paid for his work — 3s 6d(17½p) a day. The labourers were getting 1s 2d(6p). He went on to link Liverpool, Hull and Bristol together by waterway — The Grand Trunk system.

Others followed, such as the Birmingham Canal in 1768, the Droitwich Canal and Chesterfield Canal. Incredibly, Brindley never wrote anything down, he kept everything in his head. He simply went to bed to think it out! He died aged 56, on September 27th 1772.

"The Rugged Brindley has little to say for himself.
He has chained the seas together. His ships do visibly
float over valleys, and invisibly through the hearts of
mountains; the Mersey and the Thames, the Humber and the
Severn, have shaken hands."

Carlyle.

2

TRENT & MERSEY CANAL

First known as the Grand Trunk — was authorised on 14th May 1766 with a capital of £150,000. James Brindley surveyed the route — 93⅜ miles from Derwent Mouth on the Trent to Preston Brook on the Bridgewater Canal near Runcorn. Work began immediately and by 1777 the whole canal was open with 76 locks.

The principal movers in the project were Erasmus Darwin and Josiah Wedgwood who saw it as a need for the Potteries and Midlands area. The major problem in construction was the 2,900 yard long Harecastle Tunnel. Many were sceptical that the canal company would ever pay a dividend but in 1781 5% was paid and in 1825 a £100 share was worth £2,300. The canal was used considerably for the transport of clay and flint for the pottery works around Stoke on Trent. It was not until late last century that transportation rapidly declined.

The Shardlow area is covered fully in Volume One of this series. The Stoke on Trent section is particularly interesting having the remarkable Harecastle Tunnel and is described in Volume Two of this series. Volume Seven will deal with the whole of the canal from end to end — a magnificent weeks' walk!

The original Harecastle Tunnel was built by James Brindley, took eleven years to construct, and is now closed. The tunnel — 9 feet wide and 1¾ miles long — was an unprecedented undertaking in the late 18th Century. There was no towpath and horses had to be led over the hill while the boat was legged through. As a result there was a considerable time loss while boats were moved through. In 1822 Thomas Telford suggested that another tunnel be constructed next to the existing one, and this was completed in 1827 with towpath. The two tunnels then operated on a one-way system, greatly reducing the traffic conjestion. Mining subsidence gradually made Brindley's tunnel unusable and by 1918 it had been abandoned. By the 1950s the other tunnel was suffering from subsidence and part of the towpath had to be removed. Between 1973-1977 the tunnel was closed for major repairs but is once again operational. Plaques on the southern entrance record the tunnel's history and a canal milepost that once stood on the horse path is now here.

The canal is often referred to as the Grand Canal, because nine other canals radiate from it; two of them, the Coventry Canal and the Staffordshire & Worcestershire Canal, are included in this book.

WALK 1 — WILLINGTON — 2½ miles (2 walks)

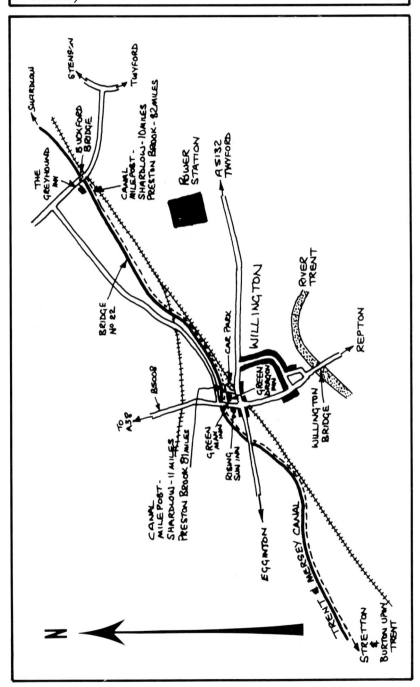

4

TRENT & MERSEY CANAL — WALK NO 1

– allow 1 hour. Two walks.

ROUTE — Willington — Trent & Mersey Canal — Buckford Bridge — and return same way.

MAP: O.S. 1:25,000 Pathfinder Series, Sheet No. SK 22/32 — Burton Upon Trent.

CAR PARK — Willington Picnic Area.

ABOUT THE WALK — With the River Trent to the south which effectively cuts off rights of way, there is little scope in the area for circular walks. However, the Trent & Mersey Canal provides delightful walking and this particular walk is to the pub and back! The towpath can be followed westwards to Stretton and the Derbyshire boundary and is again a very pleasant stroll. In both instances you return the same way.

WALKING INSTRUCTIONS — From the car park and picnic area gain the canal towpath and turn right. To your left is a canal milepost — Shardlow 11 miles; Preston Brook 81 miles. Turn right along the towpath and keep on it for just over a mile to the next milepost — Shardlow 10 miles; Preston Brook 82 miles. Just ahead is Buckford Bridge which you cross to reach The Greyhound Inn. Retrace your steps back to Willington.

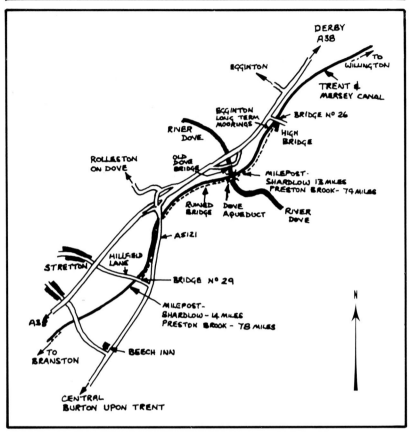

TRENT & MERSEY CANAL — WALK NO 2

3 miles — allow 1½ hours.
– the walk can be extended by a further 3 miles to include walking along the canal to Willington and its inns.

ROUTE — Hillfield Lane, Stretton — Dove Aqueduct — High Bridge (no 26) — and return same way.

MAP — O.S. 1:25,000 Pathfinder Series Sheet No SK 22/32 — Burton Upon Trent.

CAR PARK — No official one, but roadside parking on Hillfield Lane.

ABOUT THE WALK — Because of the close proximity of the dual laned A38 road and the River Trent, the area is not conducive to circular walks and you therefore have to return the same way. However, the walk can be extended to Willington in the north and to Shobnall in the south, adding 3 and 5 miles on respectively. The principal aim of this walk is to see the impressive Dove Aqueduct with views of the two road bridges over the Dove.

WALKING INSTRUCTIONS — From the canal road bridge (no. 29) descend to the canal. Just ahead is the canal milepost — Shardlow 14 miles / Preston Brook 78 miles. Return to the road bridge and walk under it and keep the canal on your left for the next 1½ miles. After ⅓ mile you pass underneath the A5121 and in just over ½ mile reach the Dove Aqueduct. Just after is another canal milepost — Shardlow 13 miles / Preston Brook 79 miles. Continue beside the canal and in another ½ mile reach High Bridge — No 26. You can continue to Willington just over 1½ miles away or retrace your steps back to Highfield Lane, Stretton where you began.

DOVE AQUEDUCT

7

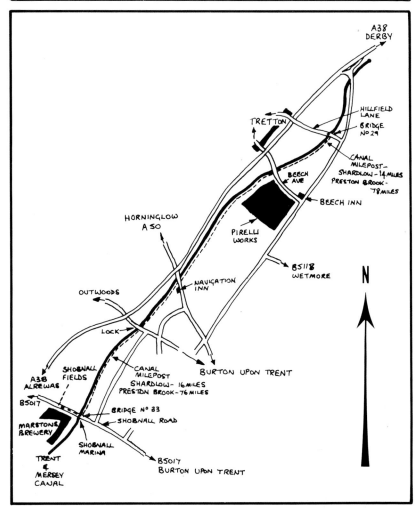

A38
DERBY

STRETTON

HILLFIELD LANE

BRIDGE No 29

CANAL MILEPOST—
SHARDLOW-14 MILES
PRESTON BROOK-
78 MILES

BEECH AVE

BEECH INN

HORNINGLOW A50

PIRELLI WORKS

B5118 WETMORE

NAVIGATION INN

N

OUTWOODS

LOCK

BURTON UPON TRENT

SHOBNALL FIELDS

A38 ALREWAS

CANAL MILEPOST
SHARDLOW- 16 MILES
PRESTON BROOK-76 MILES

B5017

BRIDGE No 33
SHOBNALL ROAD

MARSTON BREWERY

SHOBNALL MARINA

TRENT & MERSEY CANAL

B5017
BURTON UPON TRENT

SHOBNALL MARINA, BURTON UPON TRENT

TRENT & MERSEY CANAL — WALK NO 3

2½ miles one way — allow 1 hour.

ROUTE — Canal through Burton Upon Trent between Stretton and Shobnall.

MAP — O.S. 1:25,000 Pathfinder Series — Sheet No SK 22/32 — Burton Upon Trent.

CAR PARK — Roadside parking at Hillfield Lane, Stretton.
– Shobnall Fields.

ABOUT THE WALK — Lying within the heart of Burton Upon Trent it is hard to work out a circular walk which does not involve considerable road walking. As a result you simply return the same way along the canal. The walk can be used as an extension to the Stretton walk. Either way it is a pleasant walk "through the town."

WALKING INSTRUCTIONS — Starting from Hillfield Lane, Stretton or from Shobnall Fields, gain the canal and walk north to Stretton or south to Shobnall. Return the same way.

TRENT & MERSEY CANAL — HORNINGLOW

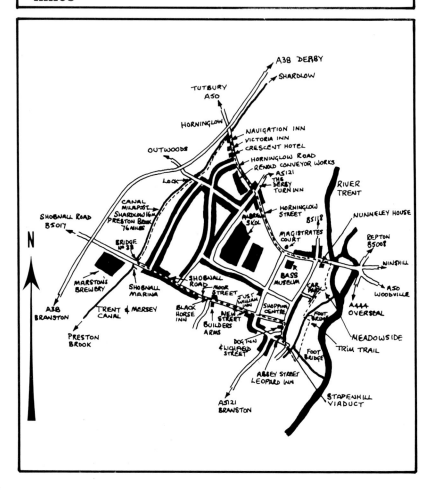

BURTON UPON TRENT — The town is synonymous with brewing but it was the monks at The Abbey founded in 1004 who discovered the local water was particularly suited to brewing. It wasn't until the 18th Century that Burton brewing became more universally well known as they could export their produce along the canal to the sea ports. In 1880 there were about 40 breweries in the town. Over the last century they have amalgamated or been taken over, and today there are just the three universally known names.

TRENT & MERSEY CANAL — WALK NO 4

4½ miles — allow 2 hours or more

ROUTE — Central Burton Upon Trent — Shobnall — Trent & Mersey Canal — Horninglow -Bass Museum — River Trent — Trent Washlands Park — Central Burton Upon.

MAP — O.S. 1:25,000 Pathfinder Series Sheet No SK 22/32 — Burton Upon Trent.

CAR PARK — The walk starts from the car park on Meadowside, but there are others adjoining the route on Green Street and just off New Street.

ABOUT THE WALK — Although based on Burton Upon Trent and walking some of its roads the walk will come as a surprise, for the area is extremely attractive, with several magnificent buildings, a delightful park with a 'trim trail'!, and, being a brewery town, an impressive brewery museum and of course, numerous inns. To complete the picture you follow a very pleasant stretch of the canal, and canal trips from Horninglow operate during the summer. There is enough to see and do here to occupy an afternoon while walking a few miles!

WALKING INSTRUCTIONS — From the car park on Meadowside, near The Library, walk away from the town — westwards — to gain a tarmaced path and the Andresey Bridge, built in 1884, over the River Trent. Bear right on the path after crossing the bridge and enter the Washlands Park, around which is a 'trim trail'. You soon walk through a children's play area and keep on the path nearest the river with the remains of an Abbey on the other side. On your left is a rugby field. In about 1/4 mile gain the walkway — Stapenhill Viaduct — and turn right along it towards the town. Keep straight ahead along Fleet Street — there is a car park on your left — and just ahead is B & Q. In front of it turn right along Abbey Street and at the end pass the 19th century London designed Leopard Inn. Continue ahead on Lichfield Street, passing the Dog Inn. Turn left along New Street — on your right is the entrance to the Burton Shopping Centre. For the next mile you keep straight ahead, first on New Street, then Moor Street and passing under the railway line, and along Shobnall Road. Upon reaching the canal bridge — No 33,- turn left down onto the towpath with Shobnall Marina on your left. Turn right along the towpath and pass under the bridge.

Keep on the towpath for the next mile passing canal milepost — Shardlow 16 miles/Preston Brook 76 miles. Next pass a lock, and a 1/3 mile later approach Horninglow and the Navigation Inn on your right. Leave the canal here and ascend to Horninglow Road. Turn right along the road, and for the next 1½ mile to the River Trent you keep straight ahead at all road junctions. First Along Horninglow Road. Pass The Derby Turn Inn and continue along Horninglow Street, passing over the railway lines, and in a 1/3 mile pass the impressive Magistrates Court on your left and reach the Bass Museum on your right. Continue ahead on Bridge Street and just before the River Trent, on your right, is Nunneley House — built in c.1760 by Samuel Sketchley, a brewer. Later it was occupied by Joseph Nunneley's Brewery. Just after the building turn right down the gradient path to regain Meadowside and car park. The tarmaced path leads round the building to the Andresey Bridge over the River Trent.

11

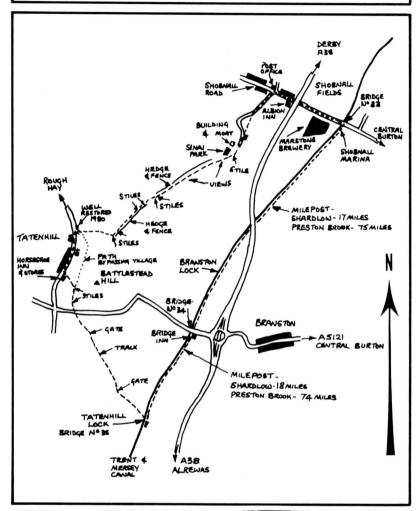

HORNINGLOW

BRANSTON — Gave its name to the famous pickle although it is not made here. Sinai Park was the summer residence of the Burton Abbey monks. The moated timber framed building dates from the 15th century.

12

TRENT & MERSEY CANAL — WALK NO 5

6 miles — allow 2½ hours

ROUTE — Branston Bridge — Trent & Mersey Canal — Tatenhill Lock — Yews Bridge — Tatenhill — Prince's Covert — Sinai Park — Shobnall — Trent & Mersey Canal — Branston Bridge.

MAP — O.S. 1:25,000 Pathfinder Series — Sheet No SK 22/32 — Burton Upon Trent.

CAR PARK — No official one, but roadside parking at Branston Bridge.

ABOUT THE WALK — A stunning walk; first beside the canal to the impressive Tatenhill Lock — cover photograph. Here you leave the canal to gain Tatenhill village, with an inn and Hall. A short but steady ascent brings you onto the ridge of Battlestead Hill, providing superlative views over Burton Upon Trent and the canal below. You follow the ridge to Sinai Park and its remarkable timber framed and moated building. From here you descend to Shobnall and walk along the road to the canal. Two miles of walking beside it passing Branston Lock returns you to Branston Bridge, and the perfectly sited canal pub, the Bridge Inn. Quite simply, a walk of exceptional character.

WALKING INSTRUCTIONS — From Branston Bridge, walk towards the inn and descend the path on the right of it to the canal. Keep ahead beside the canal on your right and pass canal milepost — Shardlow 18 miles / Preston Brook 74 miles. Little over ½ mile later gain Tatenhill Lock — bridge No 35. Ascend and turn right over the canal and follow the well defined path along the field edge on your right. Keep the field edge on your right all the way, as the path becomes a track which is well stiled and gated. A mile from the canal gain the road at Yews Bridge. Bear right to the fenced path and continue with a rock face on your right to a stile. Cross an open field to another stile and bear left up the track to the road in Tatenhill. On your left is the village stores and Horseshoe Inn.

Turn right along the road past the church, dedicated to St.Michaels & All Angels, and the impressive hall just afterwards. 150 yards later, and just before a well restored in 1980, turn right. The path along the track leads to the woodland of Battlestead Hill. Don't follow this but ascend the field and at the top head for the righthand corner of the field to the wooden stile. Ascend this and keep the field edge on your right. Soon pass a stile on your right, but don't use it. Continue along the field edge to a stile. Shortly afterwards turn right over a stile and keep the field edge on your left as you walk along the crest of the ridge towards Sinai Park, ½ mile away. Pass the farm well to the right to a stile. Continue slightly to your left to pass a very impressive moated timber framed house and shortly afterwards gain the farm road. Follow it to a solitary house on your right. Just after it continue ahead, descend the field and regain the road and follow it to Shobnall Road, opposite the Post Office. Turn right along the road for ½ mile, passing under the A38 road and past Marston's Brewery. At the canal bridge, turn right and descend to the towpath and keep the canal on your right for the next two miles back to Branston Bridge. On the way passing milepost — Shardlow 17 miles / Preston Brook 75 miles, and Branston Lock.

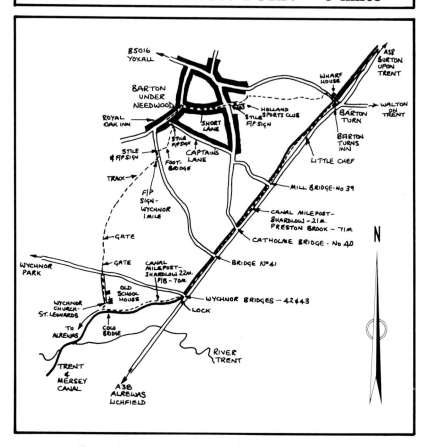

Map labels:
BS016 YOXALL
BARTON UNDER NEEDWOOD
ROYAL OAK INN
STILE & F/P SIGN
TRACK
F/P SIGN - WYCHNOR 1 MILE
SHORT LANE
STILE F/P SIGN
CAPTAINS LANE
FOOTBRIDGE
GATE
GATE
WYCHNOR PARK
CANAL MILE POST SHARDLOW 22M. F/B - 70M.
OLD SCHOOL HOUSE
WYCHNOR CHURCH- ST. LEONARDS
TO ALREWAS
COLD BRIDGE
HOLLAND SPORTS CLUB F/P SIGN
WHARF HOUSE
A38 BURTON UPON TRENT
WALTON ON TRENT
BARTON TURN
BARTON TURNS INN
LITTLE CHEF
MILL BRIDGE-No 39
CANAL MILEPOST- SHARDLOW - 21M. PRESTON BROOK - 71M.
CATHOLME BRIDGE - No 40
BRIDGE No 41
WYCHNOR BRIDGES - 42 & 43
LOCK
RIVER TRENT
A38 ALREWAS LICHFIELD
TRENT & MERSEY CANAL
N

RUFFORD No 166 — GRAND UNION CANAL CARRYING COMPANY LIMITED

BOAT NEAR GREAT HAYWOOD

BARTON UNDER NEEDWOOD — contains many brick and timber buildings. The 16th century church was a gift of John Taylor. He was one of triplets born in the village and from humble beginnings rose to be Master of the Rolls to Henry VIII.

14

TRENT & MERSEY CANAL — WALK NO 6

5 miles — allow 2 hours

ROUTE — Barton Turn — Trent & Mersey Canal — Wychnor Bridges — Wychnor — Barton Green — Barton-under-Needwood — Barton Turn.

MAPS — O.S. 1:25,000 Pathfinder Series Sheet No SK 21/31 — Ashby de la Zouch and Sheet No SK 01/11 — Rugeley and Lichfield (North).

CAR PARK — No official one, but roadside parking at Barton Turn.

ABOUT THE WALK — For the first two miles along the canal, the A38 road runs parallel to it, but despite the closeness of the road the canal is in a remarkably tranquil location. After two miles at Wychnor Bridges, the canal bears right away from the road and ¾ mile later you leave it to gain Wychnor and return to Barton Turn via Barton-under-Needwood. Where you leave the canal close to Wychnor church you can continue beside it for a further ¾ mile to cross footbridges over the River Trent and reach the attractive thatched village of Alrewas. The walk from Alrewas — Walk No 7 can also be joined via this route.

WALKING INSTRUCTIONS — From Barton Turns walk past the inn and follow the towpath, keeping the canal on your righthand side. After ¼ mile pass the Little Chef restaurant and Travelodge on your left. Keep beside the canal for the next two miles, passing bridges numbers 39 (Mill Bridge), No 40 (Catholme Bridge) and Nos 41, 42, and 43 (Wychnor). Here the canal turns right away from the road and you cross to the righthand side of the canal. ¼ mile later pass a canal milepost — Shardlow 22 miles, Preston Brook 70 miles. Keep on the right with the canal on your left passing a few small ponds on your right where mute swans nest. ½ mile from the milepost pass under Cow Bridge with Wychnor church elevated on your right. A few yards later turn right through the stile and ascend to the church.

Here gain a track and follow it past the Old School House on your right to the minor road. Go straight across and keep the hedge on your right and pass through two gates in the next ½ mile. A little after the second gate the hedge is on your lefthand side and in ½ mile you gain a track, at the end of which beside a thatched house you reach a minor road, with footpath sign — Wychnor 1 mile. Turn left and a few yards later turn right at the footpath sign and through the stile to a footbridge. Over this you bear left to the far lefthand corner of the field where there is a stile and pathsign, and the houses of Barton-under-Needwood beyond. Turn left along Captain's Lane and in a few yards gain the T junction. To your left is the Royal Oak Inn. Turn right along The Green and right again at the first road on your right — Short Lane. Keep on this for ½ mile to the next road junction. Keep straight ahead, as signed and stiled, passing a pond on your right and the grounds of Holland Sports Club. Midway between the pond and the sports pavilion, turn left over a bridge over a stream and turn right beside it to reach a footbridge in the far righthand corner. The path is now well defined and stiled as you pass a Sewage Works on your right and shortly afterwards bearing left to the road. Turn right past Wharf House and over the canal to regain Barton Turn.

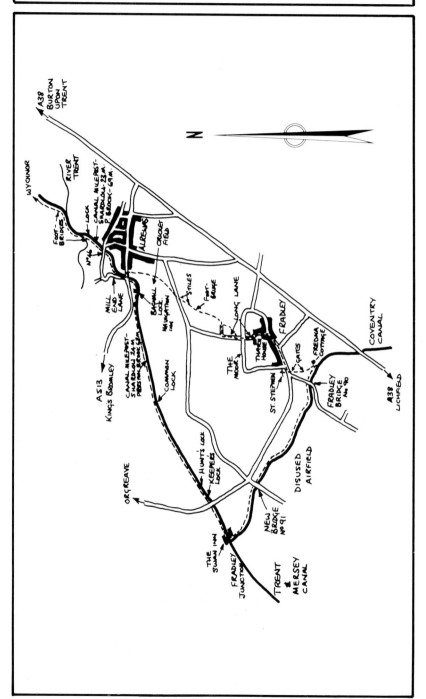

TRENT & MERSEY CANAL — WALK NO 7

6 miles — allow 2½ hours

ROUTE — Alrewas — Bagnall Lock — Trent & Mersey Canal — Fradley Junction — Coventry Canal — Fradley — Alrewas.

MAP — O.S. 1:25,000 Pathfinder Series — Sheet No SK 01/11 — Rugeley and Lichfield (North).

CAR PARK — No official one.

ABOUT THE WALK — I have begun this walk from the western side of Alrewas, at Bridge No 48, where the A513 King's Bromley road crosses the canal. Roadside parking is possible in Mill End Lane, adjacent to the bridge and canal. You can park near Fradley Junction, but this would spoil the walk! For more than two miles you walk beside the Trent and Mersey and in the final stages beside the locks to Fradley Junction — the junction of the Coventry Canal. The setting is superlative with buildings and inn overlooking the canal, and has few equals in terms of canal splendour. As a result it is best to walk here, for the first time, and appreciate the perfect location. You walk more than a mile of the Coventry Canal before walking through Fradley and over fields back to the western side of Alrewas. If time permits the walk can be extended by 1½ miles to follow the Trent and Mersey through Alrewas and over the River Trent to Wychnor — part of Walk No 6. All in all, one of my favourite canal walks!

WALKING INSTRUCTIONS — Starting from the junction of Mill End Lane and the A513 in Alrewas, descend to the canal and follow the towpath on the righthand side of it past Bagnall Lock and the Navigation Inn on your right. Shortly afterwards pass under bridge number 49 and about 1/3 mile later pass canal milepost — Shardlow 24 miles, Preston Brook 68 miles. Continue on beside the canal for another mile, passing Common Lock and then Hunt's and Keeper's Locks. Here you gain the road ajacent to the canal and in ¼ mile reach Fradley Junction. Before The Swan Inn you will have to cross over the canal to reach the Coventry Canal's towpath. Keep on the towpath for about 1½ miles, passing under bridges number 91 and 90. Just after the latter you leave the canal via a gate to the road beside cottages — Fredna Cottage. Turn left but do not follow the road; bear right to a gate and keep the field edge on your right to the next gate. At first it appears to be a private road but is a right of way; continue along the road to the road — Church Close, almost opposite St. Stephens School. There is a footpath sign at the end of the road.

Turn right along Church Close, and in just over ¼ mile in central Fradley turn left along Long Lane, past the Post Office and impressive thatched house. Cross the road — The Moor — and continue on Long Lane for a few more yards to a white painted fence on your right, which acts as a stile. Turn right over this and cross the field to the righthand corner, where there is a stile. Cross the road beyond to your right to another fence (stile) and walk round the edge of the field to your right to a footbridge in the far righthand corner. After this bear right slightly to the next two stiles to gain the road. Turn right, and a few yards later on your left is the stile and path to your right to the edge of Alrewas. At the third stile close to the houses you keep them on your right as you pass the Alrewas Cricket Ground on your left. Continue ahead across the playing field, keeping to the righthand side; to your left can be seen the canal and Navigation Inn. At the end of the field pass between the houses and gain the main road. Turn left to bridge No 48 (Kent's Bridge built in 1934) and reach your starting point. If time permits the walk to Wychnor is particularly attractive and exploring the thatched village of Alrewas and church give added enjoyment to your visit here.

ALREWAS — The church dedicated to All Saints dates from Norman times and is said to be one of the places where Lady Godiva worshipped. The village is made up of numerous timber framed buildings and is well worth exploring. The village was once famous for basket-making.

FRADLEY JUNCTION

TRENT & MERSEY NR. FRADLEY JUNCTION

TATENHILL LOCK

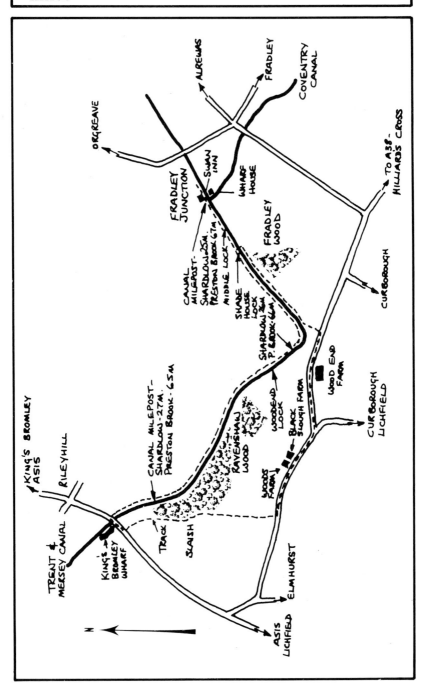

TRENT & MERSEY CANAL — WALK NO 8

5 miles — allow a little over 2 hours.

ROUTE — Fradley Junction — Trent & Mersey Canal to A515 road close to King's Bromley Wharf — Slaish Wood — Woods Farm — Wood End Farm — Trent & Mersey Canal — Shade House Lock — Fradley Junction.

MAP — O.S. 1:25,000 Pathfinder Series — Sheet No SK 01/11 — Rugeley and Lichfield (North).

CAR PARK — No official one, but roadside parking near road crossing of the canal; just north east of Fradley Junction.

ABOUT THE WALK — A really exceptional walk through remote woodland of pine, where the canal turns sharp right, heading north westerly to Rugeley. You walk along the northern side of the canal (the towpath) and in the final stages along its southern side as you return to the Swan Inn and Fradley Junction. One of my favourite canal walks anywhere — need I say more!

WALKING INSTRUCTIONS — Walk along the towpath past the Swan Inn and Fradley Junction and keep on the righthand side of the canal (northern side). Soon pass Middle Lock and shortly after Shade House Lock. This is where you rejoin your starting out path when you return from the other side of the canal. Keep on the right of the canal for the next two miles to the A515 road. After ½ mile the canal turns sharp right and a little later pass Woodend Lock. The next mile to canal milepost — Shardlow 27 miles/ Preston Brook 65 miles — is beside the woodland of Ravenshaw Wood and Slaish full of pine trees. Just after the canal milepost ascend to the A515 road bridge and on the other side is King's Bromley Wharf, the home of Lichfield Plant Services.

Turn left along the road and 50 yards later, just past the house on your left, turn left through a gate onto a track. At first the field boundary is on your left, but as the track bears right it is now on your right. Just ahead reach the woodland of Slaish entered by a stile. Continue along the track on the righthand edge and in ¼ mile gain the track to Ravenshaw House. Keep on the track to your right close to the wood's edge and in ¼ mile leave the woodland and continue on the now fenced track to a minor road. Turn left along it and keep on it for the next ¾ mile passing Woods Farm, Black Sough Farm and Wood End Farm. Near the latter you will see the canal quite clearly. Continue past the farm and descend slightly to a wooded hollow before ascending gently. After a few yards notice a stile on your right on the edge of Big Lyntus wood. A little further on your left leave the road at a gap and footbridge, and walk along the field's lefthand edge and approach the canal which, as the field bears right, you have the canal on your left. Parallel the canal to a stile and enter Fradley Wood, following a defined path beside the canal on your left. At the end of the woodland there is no stile, and at the time of writing you have to duck under a single strand of barbed wire. Keep ahead bearing right around the run off from Shad House Lock and reach a gate and track. Turn left over Bridge No 52 and turn right to retrace your steps back to the Swan Inn and Fradley Junction.

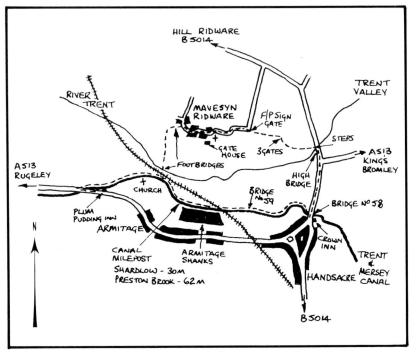

**ARMITAGE SHANKS AND
TRENT & MERSEY CANAL**

MAVESYN RIDWARE — The church has many monuments; one to the Crusader, Sir Henry Mavesyn. The gatehouse is all that remains of a Tudor manor house, built by the Mavesyn family. In Norman times the family name was Mal-voisins, meaning dangerous neighbours.

TRENT & MERSEY CANAL — WALK NO 9

4½ miles — allow 2 hours.

ROUTE — Handsacre — Trent & Mersey Canal — Armitage — Mavesyn Ridware — High Bridge — Handsacre.

MAP — O.S. 1:25,000 Pathfinder Series — Sheet No SK 01/11 — Rugeley and Lichfield (North).

CAR PARK — No official one.

ABOUT THE WALK — A delightful walk along the canal to a point where only the railway line separates the canal from the River Trent. Before leaving the canal and crossing the Trent, by continuing a short distance you can see Armitage Church on a rocky promitory and a ¼ mile later is the Plum Pudding Inn. If you do not do this extension the overall mileage of the walk is reduced to just over 3 miles. After crossing the River Trent you reach Mavesyn Ridware, a particularly attractive hamlet with an old Gate House. You cross a couple of fields to High Bridge over the Trent and a short road walk returns you to Handsacre and the canal, by an inn!

WALKING INSTRUCTIONS — The walk begins on the northern edge of Handsacre where the A513 crosses the canal close to the Crown Inn. Descend to the canal and turn right under the road bridge (No 58) and keep on the towpath with the canal on your left for the next mile. On the way you will pass under Bridge No 59 and ¼ mile later on your left is the works of Armitage Shanks with the large kilometer sign — London 195 km, Glasgow 451 km. A few yards later you pass a canal milepost — Shardlow 30 miles and Preston Brook 62 miles. In another ¼ mile you pass under Bridge no 60 and just afterwards on your right is the path which leads through a tunnel beneath the railway line to the footbridge over the River Trent. This is your route to Mavesyn Ridware, but by continuing along the canal you can see Armitage Church and further along is the Plum Pudding Inn, reached by crossing the canal just beyond.

Returning to the path and tunnel under the railway, cross the River Trent and follow the defined path towards the western side of Mavesyn Ridware. Cross a small footbridge and bear right up the fenced path to the village road beside Manor Croft. Turn right to the church dedicated to St. Nicholas, founded in 1140. To your right can be seen the ancient Gate House. Follow the road on the left of the church and pass the attractive thatched Church Cottage on your left. Continue along the lane for a little over ¼ mile and after passing two solitary houses the lane turns sharp left. Here on the corner is a footpath sign and stile covered by a hedge. Go through the gate on your right and go directly across the field to another gate followed by two others. The path line is faint but ahead you can see High Bridge over the River Trent and on its left are steps and a handrail. Aim for this, curving round the field to your right to avoid the fences. Gain the stile and ascend to the bridge. Turn right and cross the bridge and keep right on the road (A513) back to the canal and Crown Inn a little over ¼ mile away.

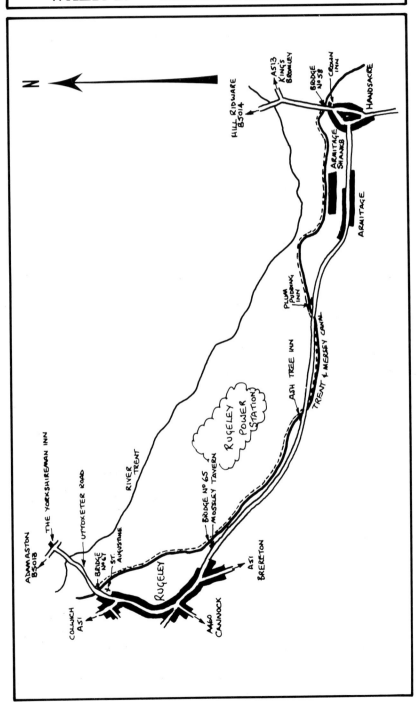

TRENT & MERSEY CANAL — WALK NO 10

4 miles — one way — allow 1½ hours.

ROUTE — Handsacre — Trent & Mersey Canal to Rugeley, where the B5013 road crosses the canal.

MAP — O.S. 1:25,000 Pathfinder Series Sheet No. SK 01/11 — Rugeley and Lichfield (North).

CAR PARKS — No official one at either end, but roadside parking is practical.

ABOUT THE WALK — The canal between Handsacre and Rugeley is sandwiched between houses of Rugeley and Brereton to the south and to the north is Rugeley Power Station. As a result there are few practical rights of way to make a circular walk other than a one way or return walk of 8 miles along the canal. Despite its closeness to these modern trappings the canal, as always, is a quiet haven and lined with inns!

WALKING INSTRUCTIONS — Starting from the A513 bridge (No 58) near the Crown Inn on the northern edge of Handsacre. Descend to the canal and turn right under the bridge and keep the canal on your lefthand side all the way to Rugeley. On the way passing Armitage Shanks works, the Plum Pudding Inn, Ash Tree Inn, and Mossley Tavern. ¾ mile later you reach Bridge No 67 — the B5013 road in Rugeley. Ascending to the road, the centre of the town is 200 yards away to your left. You can always retrace your steps back to Handsacre — you will be surprised how different the scenery looks in reverse!

PLUM PUDDING INN, ARMITAGE

25

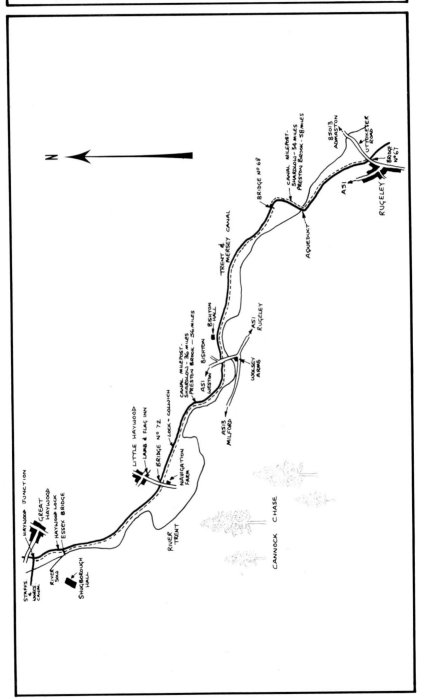

TRENT & MERSEY CANAL — WALK NO 11

5½ miles — one way — allow 2¼ hours

ROUTE — Rugeley (Bridge No 67 — the B5013) — Trent & Mersey Canal via Wolseley, Colwich, Little Haywood to Great Haywood and the junction with the Staffordshire and Worcestershire Canal — Haywood Junction.

MAPS — O.S. 1:25,000 Pathfinder Series Sheet Nos. SK 01/11 — Rugeley and Lichfield (North); No. SK 02/12 — Abbots Bromley; and No. SJ 82/92 — Stafford.

CAR PARKS — No official one at either end.

ABOUT THE WALK — A magnificent canal walk with the woodland of Cannock Chase on your left. First you cross the Rugeley Trent Aqueduct before walking along the remotest stretch to Wolseley. Afterwards houses appear on your right as you pass close to Colwich, Little Haywood and Great Haywood. Nearing the latter the impressive Shugborough Hall comes into view. The climax to the walk is Haywood Junction. You can either return the same way or do one of the other walks which link into this area. The permutations are endless!

WALKING INSTRUCTIONS — Descend to the canal beneath the B5013 Uttoxeter road — Bridge No 67. Follow the towpath on the righthand side of the canal and in less than a mile cross the Trent Aqueduct. Shortly pass canal milepost — Shardlow 34 miles/Preston Brook 58 miles. ¼ mile later at Bridge No 68 cross over, and for the rest of the walk to Haywood Junction keep the canal on your righthand side. Just beyond Haywood Junction leave the canal at the road bridge. To your right is Great Haywood.

TRENT & MERSEY CANAL AT RUGELEY

27

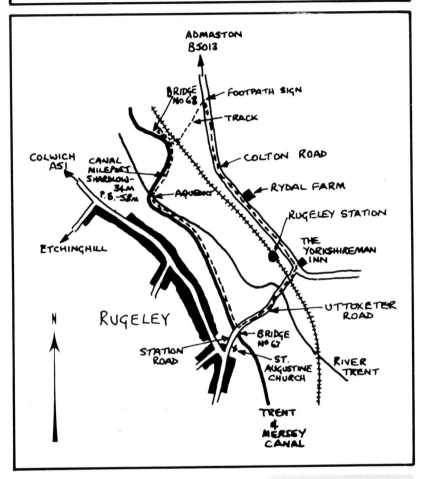

ADMASTON
B5013

BRIDGE No 68

FOOTPATH SIGN

TRACK

COLWICH A51

CANAL MILEPOST
SHARDLOW—
34M
P.B.—58M

COLTON ROAD

AQUEDUCT

RYDAL FARM

RUGELEY STATION

THE YORKSHIREMAN INN

ETCHINGHILL

N

RUGELEY

UTTOXETER ROAD

STATION ROAD

BRIDGE No 67

ST. AUGUSTINE CHURCH

RIVER TRENT

TRENT & MERSEY CANAL

**ABANDONED
RUGELEY CHURCH**

TRENT & MERSEY CANAL — WALK NO 12

3 miles — allow 1¼ hours.

ROUTE — Bridge No 67 (B5013 Uttoxeter Road) Rugeley — Trent & Mersey Canal — Trent Aqueduct — Bridge No 68 — B5013 road — Rugeley Station — Bridge No 67.

MAP — O.S. 1:25,000 Pathfinder Series Sheet No SK 01/11 — Rugeley and Lichfield (North).

CAR PARK — No official one, but roadside parking on Station Road, near St. Augustine's church.

ABOUT THE WALK — A short walk to see the Trent Aqueduct. The canal in this part of Rugeley is particularly attractive. To return you walk along a minor road and pass the Yorkshireman Inn.

WALKING INSTRUCTIONS — From Station Road descend to the canal from the B5013 Uttoxeter road. Walk under the bridge on the towpath keeping the canal on your left. In almost a mile the canal turns sharp right and you cross the River Trent via the aqueduct. Shortly afterwards pass canal milepost — Shardlow 34 miles/Preston Brook 58 miles. ¼ mile later at the next canal bridge — No 68 — leave the canal and turn right onto a track which doubles back on your route before turning left over the railway line and on to the B5013 road. There is a right of way across the field on your right but it is usually impractical to follow because of ploughing. It is simpler and easier to continue to the road and turn right along it. Pass Rydal Farm and ¼ mile later turn right under the railway line — on your right is Rugeley Railway Station and on your left the Yorkshireman Inn. Continue along the B5013 road over the River Trent and back to Bridge No 67 where you began. A few yards from the bridge towards Rugeley town centre is St. Augustines Church on your left and the largely ruined one on your right, which is well worth looking at.

TRENT AQUEDUCT, RUGELEY

RUGELEY — The church fell into a poor condition and was abandoned, although the tower and arches remain. The 13th Century chapel still remains in good condition. Across the road a new church was built last century. The town, which was granted a charter in 1259, has a popular market.

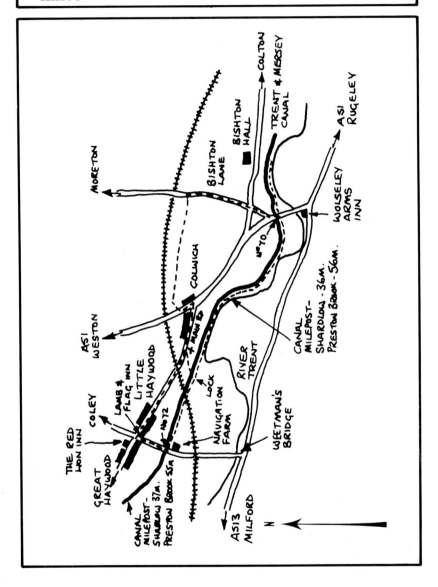

TRENT & MERSEY CANAL WALK NO 13

4 miles — allow 1½ hours.

ROUTE — Little Haywood — Trent & Mersey Canal — Wolseley — Bishton — Colwich — Little Haywood.

MAP — O.S. 1:25,000 Pathfinder Series — Sheet No SK 02/12 — Abbots Bromley.

CAR PARK — No official one.

ABOUT THE WALK — Exploring a small section of the canal between Little Haywood and Wolseley, with the River Trent close by. You return via Bishton and views of its hall before following a little used right of way to Colwich. Here you can either walk along the road into Little Haywood or return to the canal at Colwich Lock. There are two inns in Little Haywood and another ¼ mile from the route — Wolseley Arms — where you leave the canal for Bishton. A delightful short walk with the wooded slopes of Cannock Chase close by.

WALKING INSTRUCTIONS — From the crossroads in Little Haywood, close to the Lamb & Flag Inn, turn left along Meadow Lane. Pass under the railway bridge and pass Navigation Farm on your right and reach the canal bridge, No 72. Descend to your left down to the canal and continue along the towpath with the canal on your left. In just under ½ mile reach Colwich Lock and bridge No 71. Here the path from near Colwich Church joins the canal and is an optional return route. Continue along the canal with the River Trent on your immediate right. Pass canal mile post — Shardlow 36 miles/ Preston Brook 56 miles. ½ mile later reach the A51 road bridge — No 70 and ascend to the road. If you continue along the canal a short distance you can see Bishton Hall on your left.

Turn left across the bridge — to your right is the Wolseley Arms. Turn right almost immediately along the lane towards Bishton. At the cross roads in less than ¼ mile cross over and follow Bishton Lane. Keep on this for about ⅓ mile and at the start of the last field before the railway, leave the road at a wooden fence. The stile was not here on my walk. Keep the hedge/fence on your right to gain the next wooden fence/stile. Continue towards the end of the next field still keeping the hedge/fence on your right. Near the far corner is another wooden fence/stile. Ascend this and turn left immediately, keeping the field boundary now on your lefthand side. Reach a gate and cross the next field to a stile. Here gain a track and follow it to your left then right around the farm buildings to the A51 road. Turn left then right along the Village road past the village store in Colwich. Just past the church on your left is the stile and track back to the canal. Those heading for Little Haywood continue on the Main Road and pass St. Mary's Abbey on your right before reaching the crossroads where you began close to the Lamb & Flag Inn. Just ahead is the Red Lion Inn on your right.

WALK 14 — SEVEN SPRINGS — 7 miles

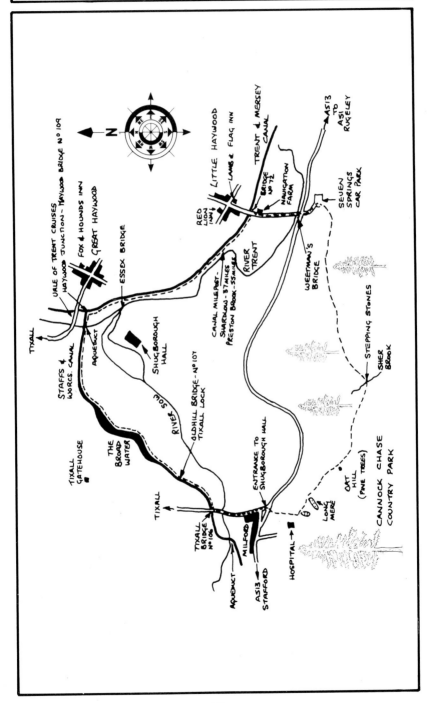

SEVEN SPRINGS CAR PARK

A513 TO RUGELEY

TRENT & MERSEY CANAL

LITTLE HAYWOOD

LAMB & FLAG INN

BRIDGE No 72

NAVIGATION FARM

RED LION INN

WEETMAN'S BRIDGE

RIVER TRENT

CANAL MILEPOST — SHARDLOW - 37 MILES — PRESTON BROOK - 55 MILES

STEPPING STONES

SHER BROOK

VALE OF TRENT CRUISES — HAYWOOD JUNCTION — HAYWOOD BRIDGE No 109

FOX & HOUNDS INN

GREAT HAYWOOD

ESSEX BRIDGE

SHUGBOROUGH HALL

TIXALL

STAFFS & WORCS. CANAL

AQUEDUCT

OLDHILL BRIDGE - No 107 TIXALL LOCK

RIVER SOW

ENTRANCE TO SHUGBOROUGH HALL

TIXALL GATEHOUSE

THE BROAD WATER

TIXALL

CANNOCK CHASE COUNTRY PARK

OAT HILL (PINE TREES)

LONG MERE

TIXALL BRIDGE No 106

MILFORD

HOSPITAL

AQUEDUCT

A513 STAFFORD

32

TRENT & MERSEY CANAL — WALK NO 14

7 miles — allow 2½ to 3 hours.

ROUTE — Seven Springs Car Park — Trent & Mersey Canal — Haywood Junction — Staffordshire & Worcestershire Canal — Tixall Bridge — Milford Common — Oat Hill — Cannock Chase — Stepping Stones — Seven Springs.

MAPS — O.S. 1:25,000 Pathfinder Series Sheets No SK 02/12 — Abbots Bromley, and No SJ 82/92 — Stafford.

CAR PARKS — Seven Springs — Grid Ref. SK 005206.
— Milford Common.

ABOUT THE WALK — Quite simply, a stunning walk. First along the Trent & Mersey Canal with views of Shugborough Hall before gaining the junction with the Staffordshire & Worcester Canal. Along here you pass the unusually wide Broad Water and views of Tixall. You leave the canal at Tixall Bridge to reach Cannock Chase. Here a splendid walk through woodland and open spaces returns you to Seven Springs. I first did this walk in perfect weather in January and whilst the walk was among the finest canal walks I have ever done, I was fortunate to see a kingfisher with a fish in its beak on the Trent & Mersey Canal near Great Haywood.

WALKING INSTRUCTIONS — Starting from Seven Springs car park descend the track back to the main road — A513. Cross over onto the minor road to Little Haywood and soon cross Weetman Bridge over the River Trent. Shortly after passing under the railway bridge you reach the canal bridge (No 72). Turn right down to the canal and turn left under the bridge and keep on the towpath with the canal (Trent & Mersey) on your right. In ¼ mile pass canal milepost — Shardlow 37 miles, Preston Brook 55 miles. Keep beside the canal for the next mile, with views of Shugborough Hall, before reaching Haywood Junction. Don't cross the bridge (No 109) but turn left under it to begin walking along the towpath of the Staffordshire & Worcestershire Canal.

HAYWOOD JUNCTION

33

Again keeping the canal on your right, cross an aqueduct and ½ mile later pass Broad Water, often inhabited with mute swans. A further ½ mile brings you to Oldhill Bridge and Tixall Lock. Little over ¼ mile later gain Tixall Bridge, No 107. Here leave the canal and turn left along the road, over the River Sow and railway line to Milford Common — on your right, and the Entrance Gates to Shugborough Hall on your left. Cross the A513 road bearing right to a well defined track and enter Cannock Chase. This curves round to your right before leading you gently up to a cluster of pine trees. A few yards later reach a cross roads of paths/tracks with a hospital a little to your right. Turn left and descend slightly to a small lake on your right and continue ahead ascending and descending to another — Long Mere. Continue ascending and in ¼ mile gain the crest of Oat Hill. A little to your right is a small fenced enclosure of pine trees. Keep to the path a little to your left to walk through pine trees before descending steeply to another crossroads of tracks. Keep ahead on the defined track, signposted — Stepping Stones ¾ mile, although it is not as far as that! In ½ mile reach the stepping stones and turn left across them, now following a signed path — Seven Springs. It is 1½ miles to these and after nearly ¾ mile keep to the lefthand path in open country and ignore all side trails. Eventually the path, which has been in a shallow valley all the time, curves left to Seven Springs and its car park and picnic tables.

CANNOCK CHASE — once a very large royal hunting forest, approximately 3,000 acres of woodlands and heath are now a Country Park managed by the Staffordshire County Council. The surrounding forest, which covers 6,700 acres, is one of the oldest forests in Britain.

SHUGBOROUGH HALL — National Trust property and the country seat of the well known photographer, Patrick Lichfield. The Mansion House was built in the 17th and 18th century.

ESSEX BRIDGE — named after the Earls of Essex, it once had more than 40 arches. Today there are only 14 of the original left. It is the longest packhorse bridge in England.

TIXALL GATE HOUSE AND THE STAFFORDSHIRE & WORCESTER-SHIRE CANAL

WALK 15 — GREAT HAYWOOD — 5 miles

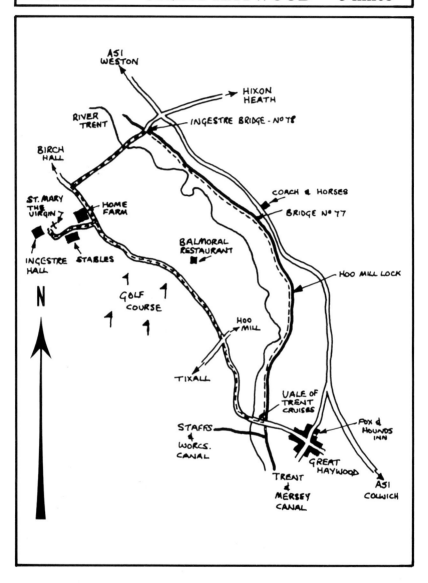

INGESTRE — The Hall dates from 1604 and was rebuilt in 1882 following a fire. It was one of the Earls of Shrewsbury residences. The small 17th Century church built in 1676 was designed by Sir Christopher Wren and is regarded as being one of the finest outside London. Inside are monuments to the Chetwynds and Talbots which are believed to be the work of Gibbons.

TRENT & MERSEY CANAL — WALK NO 15

5 miles — allow 2¼ hours.

ROUTE — Great Haywood — Trent & Mersey Canal — Ingestre Bridge No 78 — Ingestre Church — Ingestre — Great Haywood.

MAP — O.S. 1:25,000 Pathfinder Series Sheet No SJ 82/92 — Stafford.

CAR PARK — No official one.

ABOUT THE WALK — You walk beside the canal for little over two miles to Bridge No. 78. Here you leave it to gain Ingestre Hall — now an Arts Centre — an impressive mansion with a 17th century church opposite. You return to Great Haywood along roads. There is no inn actually on the walk but the Coach & horses Inn is just off the canal at Bridge 77 and another is in Great Haywood.

WALKING INSTRUCTIONS — From the bridge over the canal descend to the towpath and walk beside the canal, on your right as you head northwards, passing almost immediately the Vale of Trent Cruises. After a mile reach Hoo Mill Lock and in a further ½ mile Bridge 77. Under a mile later leave the canal at Ingestre Bridge No 78. Turn left along the track and cross the River Trent. ½ mile later at the T junction turn left and walk along the track past Home Farm to the tarmaced road. Turn right to pass the former Stable block to reach Ingestre Church dedicated to St. Mary the Virgin; opposite is the Hall. Retrace your steps and keep on the tarmaced road past the houses of Ingestre, golf course, and turn off to the Balmoral Restaurant. ½ mile later reach the Tixall/Great Haywood road. Bear left along it and in ¾ mile cross the River Trent and regain the canal.

STABLES, INGESTRE HALL

37

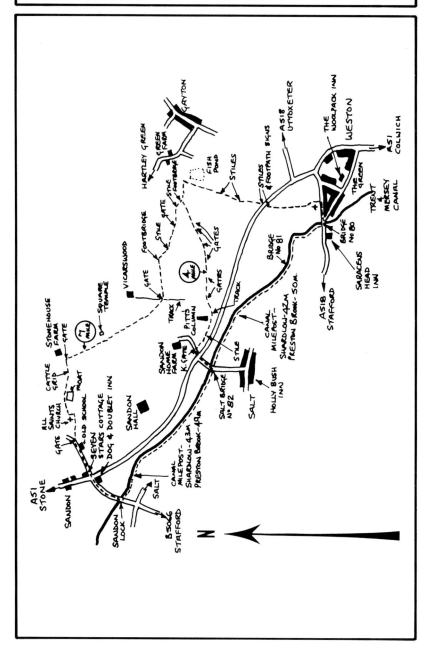

TRENT & MERSEY CANAL — WALK NOS 16 & 17

4 and 7 miles — allow 2 and 3 hours.

ROUTE — Weston — Trent & Mersey Canal — Salt Bridge — Sandon Lock — Sandon Church — Sandon Upper Park — Chair Plantation — Fish Pond near Moat Farm, Gayton — A51 — Weston.

- the shorter route goes from Salt Bridge direct via Pitts Column to the Fish Pond.

MAP — O.S. 1:25,000 Pathfinder Series Sheet No SJ 82/92 — Stafford.

CAR PARK — No official one.

ABOUT THE WALKS — A dramatic piece of canal walking with rolling wooded hills on either side. A mile along the canal and ahead can be seen Pitts Column. The shorter walk leaves the canal at the splendidly built Salt Bridge, and passes beneath the column, before crossing fields to the Fish Pond. The longer walk takes you across the Sandon estate with views of the hall. The pathline is there but little used. There are inns in Weston and another near the halfway point at the A51 road in Sandon.

WALKING INSTRUCTIONS — 7 mile walk — On the western side of Weston leave the A518 road near the Saracen's Head Inn and gain the towpath. Turn left along it passing under the A518 road bridge (No 80) and keep the canal on your right for the next two miles — one mile to Salt Bridge for the shorter walk. Pass under Sandhill Bridge (No 81) and ½ mile later pass canal milepost — Shardlow 42 miles, Preston Brook 50 miles. Little over ¼ mile later gain Salt Bridge, No 82. For the shorter walk instructions see separate details below. Continue beside the canal and in ¾ mile pass canal milepost — Shardlow 43 miles, Preston Brook 49 miles. From here you are in sight of Sandon Lock where you leave the canal and turn right over the bridge. Cross the railway bridge and reach the A51 road beside the Dog and Doublet Inn.

Cross the A51 road and walk up the No Through Road; on your immediate right are the entrance gates to Sandon Hall. ¼ mile along the lane and just past the old school on your right the lane bears left. Keep ahead to a gate and cross the field heading for the white painted gate on the right of the churchyard. Walk around All Saints church to your left to another white gate. Turn right and cross the grassland cutting the corner off the track to gain it on the right of buildings at a T junction. Cross the track and keep on the other one passing a moat and building on your right. Beyond this you cross a cattle grid and almost opposite Stonehouse Farm on your left leave the track and go through a gate into the Upper Park of Sandon Estate. The pathline is faint but simply aim for the righthand side of the wood ahead. Continue past this and still in open country keep a square temple well to your left and the edge of another wood well to your right. ¼ mile from the temple and opposite an enclosure on the wood edge, you begin bearing left slightly and soon descend to a track having skirted round a hollow. Cross the track to a gate and keep the hedge on your lefthand side. Near the end of the field go through a gap and keep the hedge on your right to a wooden fence. There is no stile here but cross over and almost immediately cross a flat bridge over a stream. Turn right and soon reach a stile in the fence on your left, followed by a footbridge. Keep straight ahead to a gate with a pond on your left. Keep the hedge on your left as you walk along the edge of the field to a stile. It is here that the shorter route joins the main route.

Over the stile bear right slightly to a footbridge and then straight ahead aiming for the church of Gayton. But don't exit the field! After 50 yards bear right and you can see the fishpond on your left. At the field boundary are two wooden bars acting as a stile. Over this continue ahead to a solitary tree beside a stile. Cross the next field to another stile, footpath sign — Gayton 1 mile — and the A51 road. Cross over to another stile and path sign — Weston — and keep the stream on your left at first to the railway line. Over this keep the stream on your right and where it curves right keep ahead towards the lefthand side of Weston Church. Cross a footbridge and walk past the church to the road. Turn right to regain the canal and the Saracen's Head. Just before the canal on your left is The Green and a little way along here is the Woolpack Inn.

4 mile walk — Leave the canal at Salt Bridge — No 82. Turn right over the bridge to the A51 road. Cross over and walk past the lodge along the road to Sandon Home Farm. In a few yards turn right at the kissing gate and ascend to a stile and track. Bear right along it, crossing a cattle grid almost immediately, and keep to the lefthand track which curves round in woodland beneath Pitt's Column. A little later the track divides again but keep to the righthand one and descend to the wood edge with a pond on your right. Go through the gate directly ahead keeping the woodland and field edge on your immediate right. At the end of the field is another gate. Cross the next field to the lefthand side of a small wood where there is a gate. Continue ahead across the next field to another gate. Bear slightly left now across the field aiming for the righthand side of another wood. Again there is a gate. Bear right and before the next gate ascend the fence on your left — there is no stile here. Cross the next field to its top righthand corner to a stile. Here the longer route joins the route and you cross the stile, shortly afterwards a footbridge and on towards the Fish Pond.

TRENT & MERSEY CANAL AND PITTS MONUMENT

SALT BRIDGE

SANDON LOCK

WALK 18 — ASTON — 4 miles

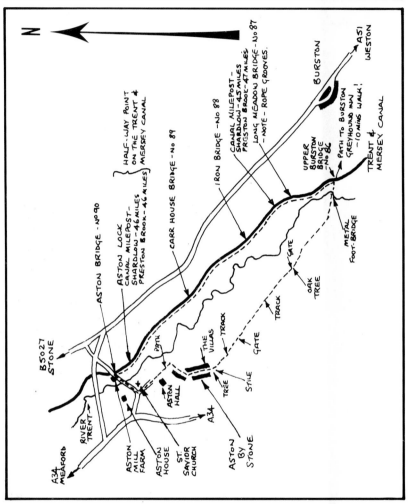

FOOTBRIDGE NEAR UPPER BURSTON OVER RIVER TRENT

TRENT & MERSEY CANAL — WALK NO 18

4 miles — allow 1½ hours.

ROUTE — Aston Bridge — Aston Hall — Trent Valley — Upper Burston Bridge — Trent & Mersey Canal — Aston Bridge.

MAP — O.S. 1:25,000 Pathfinder Series Sheet No SJ 83/93 Stone (Staffs).

CAR PARK — No official one.

ABOUT THE WALK — A delightful canal walk between the hamlets of Burston and Aston. I have started the walk from Aston Bridge — the northern end of the walk but you can start from Burston — The Greyhound Inn there is only "10 minutes walk along the lane" from the canal! The major attraction of the walk is reaching the halfway point on the Trent & Mersey Canal at Aston Lock.

WALKING INSTRUCTIONS — From Aston Bridge — No 90 — walk down the lane past Aston Mill Farm and cross the River Trent and ascend to the T junction near the church. Turn left and in a few yards, as indicated by the Public Footpath sign, walk along Aston Grange Road, with Aston Hall and its road on your right. Past the houses on your left gain a stile and defined path. In a few yards you turn sharp right now on a track and pass more houses — Glanaron. The track soon becomes a road and bears left past the houses of Aston. Where the road turns sharp right, close to a tree and house, The Villas, you keep ahead to the stile and track. Follow this track across the fields to a gate in ¼ mile. Beyond keep on the track to the end of the next field ½ mile away. Here the track ends. Go through the gate beside the oak tree. The pathline is now undefined and the field is often full of crops. It is easier to walk around the field edge aiming for the far lefthand corner of the field. There is no stile here, but once over the fence bear left to the metal footbridge over the River Trent. A few yards later and you are at the canal at bridge No 86 — Upper Burston Bridge. The towpath is on the lefthand side of the canal. As signed the Greyhound Inn is — "10 minutes walk to the top of the lane!"

You now walk beside the canal for the next 1¾ miles back to Aston Bridge. On the way pass under Long Meadow Bridge — No 87, which has some excellent rope grooves. Soon afterwards pass canal milepost — Shardlow 45 miles, Preston Brook 47 miles. ¼ mile pass under the Iron Bridge — No 88. A further ½ mile Carr House Bridge — No 89. In another ½ mile gain Aston Lock and the canal milepost — Shardlow 46 miles, Preston Brook 46 miles. The halfway point on the Trent & Mersey Canal. A short distance more and you are back at Aston Bridge.

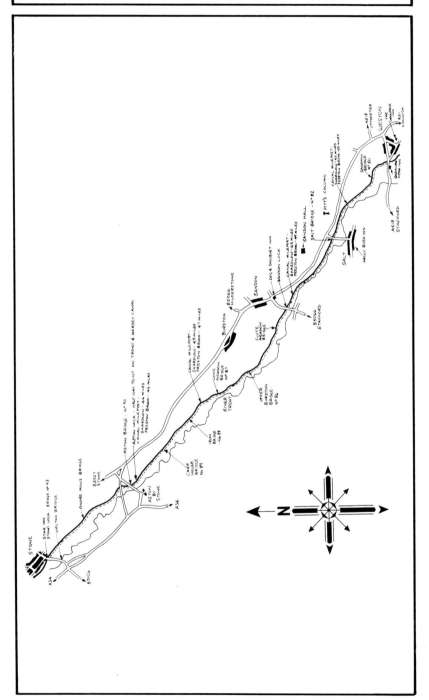

TRENT & MERSEY CANAL — WALK NO 19

ONE WAY — 7 miles — allow 2½ hours.

ROUTE — Weston — Trent & Mersey Canal — Stone.

MAPS — O.S. 1:25,000 Pathfinder Series Sheet Nos SJ 82/92 — Stafford and Sheet No SJ 83/93 — Stone (Staffs).

CAR PARKS — Weston — No official one.
- Stone — several in close promimity to the town centre.

ABOUT THE WALK & WALKING INSTRUCTIONS — A really superb canal walk which can be started from either end. Whilst it is a one way walk there is nothing to stop you from doing it as a circular one of 14 miles, walking back along the canal to your start. Beginning at Weston you have the stretch beneath Sandon Estate with the Pitt's Column as a landmark before gaining the impressive Salt Bridge. A mile later is Sandon Lock before the remoter section through the Trent Valley past Burston to Aston. The final section from here to Stone becomes more built up and the canal in Stone is very impressive especially around The Star Inn and neighbouring locks. Because there are no really suitable rights of way in the Stone and Salt area to make circular walks, this walk enables you to explore more fully this section of the canal.

STAR INN AND LOCKS, STONE

45

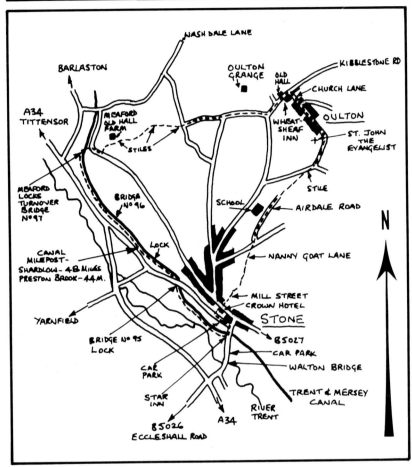

TRENT & MERSEY CANAL AND MEAFORD LOCKS

TRENT & MERSEY CANAL — WALK NO 20

5 miles — allow 2¼ hours.

ROUTE — Stone — Trent & Mersey Canal — Stone Locks — Meaford Locks — Meaford Old Hall Farm — Outlanes — Oulton — Stone via Nanny Goat Lane.

MAP — O.S. 1:25,000 Pathfinder Series Sheet No SJ 83/93 — Stone (Staffs).

CAR PARKS — Central Stone and near Walton Bridge.

ABOUT THE WALK — A superlative canal walk through Stone and its numerous locks. From the Meaford Locks you leave the canal and ascend to the village of Oulton before descending through attractive scenery back to Stone and the canal. The walk can be joined to the Meaford/Tittensor walk (No 21) making a circuit of 12 miles.

WALKING INSTRUCTIONS — Starting from the Star Inn in Stone, by bridge No 93, walk past the inn to the towpath and turn left. Keep the canal on your right. Soon pass the Trent Hospital on your left and in the next ½ mile pass two locks before reaching canal milepost — Shardlow 48 miles, Preston Brook 44 miles. ¾ mile later gain Meaford Lock and Bridge No 97, a Turnover Bridge. Here you ascend to the other side — righthand side of the canal, but don't follow it! This is where the Tittensor walk joins. After crossing the bridge keep ahead on the road and in 20 yards turn left down what looks like a private drive and pass under a railway bridge. Keep to the right of Meaford Old Hall Farm as stiled and soon walk along a fenced track. At the next stile you keep the hedge on your right and at the end of the field reach a stile and road junction on your left. Turn left then right almost immediately and pass Outlanes on your left. ¼ mile later at the cross-roads keep ahead with Oulton Grange well to your left.

At the next road junction turn left along Kibblestone Road. Pass the Old Hall on your left and the inns — Brushmaker's Arms and Wheatsheaf Inn — before turning right along Church Lane in Oulton. Follow this past the houses and Post Office and the church dedicated to St. John the Evangelist. Just after the road turns right and in ¼ mile at the T junction cross to your right to a stile and follow the defined stiled and path-signed path to Airdale Road. Follow this past the school on your right to a main road. Cross to your right and walk along Nanny Goat Lane. Follow it down to a lane, keeping to your left of the houses. A few yards later turn left and cross the bridge over the railway line. Now as you approach central Stone, turn left at the bottom and right along Mill Street to the main shopping area. Cross the road to your right and pass the Market Place and on past the Old Fire Station Bookshop. Opposite is a car park. To your left a short distance down the road is the Star Inn.

STONE — Market town with a market on Tuseday

BOAT NEAR GREAT HAYWOOD

CARRYING BOAT NEAR STONE

TRENT & MERSEY CANAL, WOODEND LOCK

COVENTRY CANAL NEAR HUDDLESFORD

49

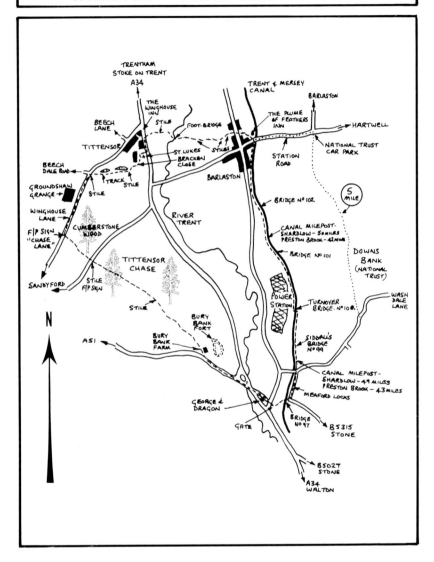

Turn left and descend the A51 road to Meaford and its junction of the A34 road with Yesterday's Inn in the centre. Keep to the righthand side to cross the A34 road and in a few yards left along the road past the Beefeater Inn — George & Dragon. Turn left along the Barlaston road and right almost immediately up a track to a wooden gate. Through this continue along the track to the bridge over the canal, close to where you began.

TRENT & MERSEY CANAL — WALK NO 21

7 miles — allow 2½ to 3 hours.

ROUTE — Meaford Locks — Trent & Mersey Canal — Barlaston — River Trent — Tittensor — Groundslow Fields — Winghouse Lane — Cumberstone Wood — Tittensor Chase — Bury Bank Farm — Meaford — Meaford Locks.

MAP — O.S. 1:25,000 Pathfinder Series Sheet No SJ 83/93 — Stone (Staffs).

CAR PARK — No official one.

ABOUT THE WALK — A longer one than usual but one of tremendous character. First beside the canal and several locks and a turnover bridge and on to lower Barlaston. Here you cross the fields to a bridge over the River Trent to reach Tittensor. After passing the houses you descend to a series of mill ponds. A short road walk brings you to woodland and the walk through Tittensor Chase on an excellent path. You descend to Meaford and after passing a couple of inns regain the canal. Whilst this walk circles the western side of the canal, a further walk of 5 miles altogether can be done by turning eastwards at Lower Barlaston and ascending to Barlaston. At the crossroads turn right to a small National Trust car park and follow the path over Down Banks to Wash Dale Lane. Turn right down this and regain the canal at Meaford Locks.

WALKING INSTRUCTIONS — From Meaford Locks walk along the righthand side of the canal past Siddall's Bridge — No 99 — and a little over ¼ mile later reach the Turnover Bridge — No 100. Here cross over and, for the rest of the walk to the road at Barlaston 1½ miles away, keep to the lefthand side. Leave the road at Barlaston close to the Plume of Feathers Inn. Turn left past the inn and right almost immediately "to Station Road." In a few yards turn left between houses 35 and 37 on the path. At the road beyond cross to your right to the footpath — "Barlaston to Tittensor. The path is well stiled and after the second one you keep the field edge on your left. After the next stile the footbridge can be seen ahead over the River Trent. Cross over and bear right to ascend round woodland to a stile. Continue ahead to the A34 road.

Turn left and in a few yards cross over and walk through the churchyard of St. Lukes Church to a road. Turn left along Bracken Close. At the end close to house No 43 leave the road onto a path and bear right and descend through woodland to a stile and mill pond on your right. Ascend a brief distance before turning right with the ponds to your right. The pathline is now a defined track which you follow to Winghouse Lane, ¼ mile away. Turn left up the lane past Groundslow Grange on your right and ¼ mile later at the other side of woodland is the footpath sign — "To Chase Lane". The path is well defined through the sparse woodland to the lane less than ½ mile away. Cross the lane to the next stile and footpath sign. Again this is a splendid path through woodland of Tittensor Chase. After ¾ mile you gain a stile and open fields. Again the pathline is obvious, and after the first field you keep the field edge on your right as you head for Bury Bank Farm. Upon gaining the farm drive, cross it to your right and in the far corner of the "field" is a stile and path sign.

WALK 22 — BARLASTON — 3½ miles

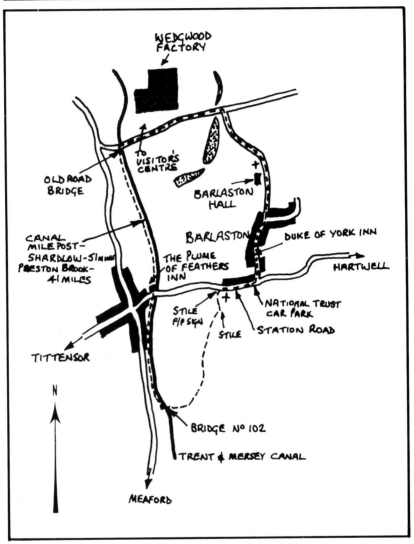

WEDGWOOD FACTORY

TO VISITORS CENTRE

OLD ROAD BRIDGE

BARLASTON HALL

CANAL MILE POST — SHARDLOW - 51 MILES PRESTON BROOK - 41 MILES

BARLASTON

DUKE OF YORK INN

HARTWELL

THE PLUME OF FEATHERS INN

NATIONAL TRUST CAR PARK

STILE F/P SIGN

STILE

STATION ROAD

TITTENSOR

N

BRIDGE No 102

TRENT & MERSEY CANAL

MEAFORD

BARLASTON HALL

TRENT & MERSEY CANAL — WALK NO 22

3½ miles — allow 1½ hours.

ROUTE — Barlaston (Lower nr the Plume of Feathers Inn) — Trent & Mersey Canal — Oldroad Bridge — Wedgewood Factory — Barlaston Hall — Barlaston — Trent & Mersey Canal — Lower Barlaston.

MAP — O.S. 1:25,000 Pathfinder Series Sheet No SJ 83/93 — Stone (Staffs).

CAR PARK — No official one.

ABOUT THE WALK — A delightful stretch of the canal with a section at the beginning and end of the walk. As you pass the Wedgewood Factory a visit to it is well worthwhile before ascending to the attractive Barlaston Hall. You descend through fields back to the canal leaving a ½ mile walk beside it back to the start.

WALKING INSTRUCTIONS — Starting from Lower Barlaston near the Plume of Feathers Inn, gain the towpath and head due north keeping the canal on your righthand side. In just over ¼ mile pass the canal milepost — Shardlow 51 miles, Preston Brook 41 miles. Little over ⅓ mile later reach Oldroad Bridge — No 104. Here leave the canal and turn right over the bridge and follow the road to the railway crossing. Beyond you will see the sign — Footpath to Visitor's Centre, with Wedgewood's Factory prominent. Keep on the road and from it you will see on your left the monument to Josiah Wedgewood. ¼ mile later turn right up the curving right towards Barlaston Church and Hall, both of which you pass on your righthand side. Continue on to the road and keep ahead through the village past the Post Office and Duke of York Inn. At the end of the road, with the National Trust Car Park ahead, turn right down Station Road. Just past the new church on your left turn left at the stile and footpath sign. The path is defined as you contour round to another stile. Just after this you bear right and descend across the fields with the hedge on your right and cross the railway line. Just afterwards cross Bridge No 102 over the canal and gain the towpath. Keep the canal on your right and walk past the houses on your left back to Barlaston and the Plume of Feathers Inn.

WEDGWOOD VISITOR'S CENTRE — The Centre is passed on the Barlaston walk and can also be gained from the canal at Bridge No 104, where pedestrian signs guide you. The museum traces the development of Wedgwood from 1759 to the present day by displays and an award winning film. The Crafts Demonstration Hall enables the visitor to see at first hand the creation of the fabled ware and the many skilled processes that are entailed in its production.

BARLASTON HALL — Palladian house built in 1756 by Robert Taylor for Thomas Mills, an attorney in Leek. The building, which has been extensively restored, is a Grade One listed building.

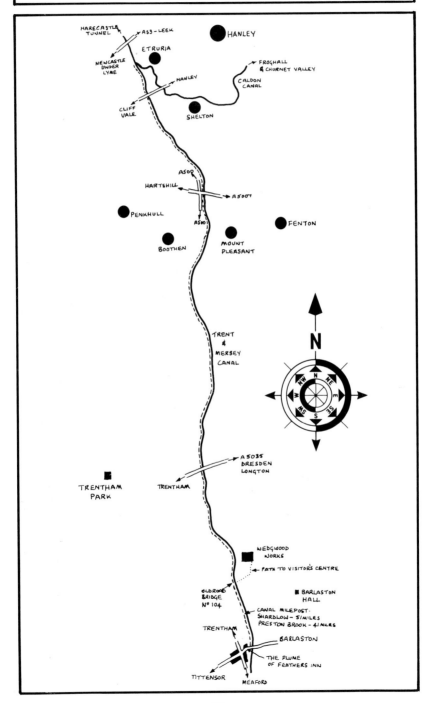

TRENT & MERSEY CANAL — WALK NO 23

5 miles — one way — allow 2¼ hours.

ROUTE — Barlaston — Wedgwood Factory — Trentham — Etruria.

MAPS — O.S. 1:25,000 Pathfinder Series Sheet Nos SJ 83/93 — Stone (Staffs) and Sheet No SJ 84/94 — Stoke on Trent.

CAR PARKS — No official ones.

ABOUT THE WALK & WALKING INSTRUCTIONS — The walk begins at the Plume of Feathers Inn, Barlaston, and ends at Etruria at the junction of the Caldon Canal. It is a one way walk as the canal passes through heavily built up areas of The Potteries, meaning there are no rights of way for circular routes apart from road walking. I tried to link it with Trentham Gardens but again there was too much road walking and I abandoned the plan. The walk is very enjoyable despite the industrial and suburbia sprawl, for as always the canal is a haven carving its way through the metropolis. You start in rural landscape and pass the Wedgwood Factory on the other side of the canal. Next you pass through Trentham, and not long afterwards you begin passing the many towns that make up The Potteries. Etruria is the junction of the Caldon Canal and this is covered fully by my Vol Two of Canal Walks. You can always retrace your steps back to Barlaston, making a 10 mile walk, or even set off along the Caldon Canal!

TRENT AND MERSEY CANAL AND WEDGWOOD FACTORY

WALK 24 — END TO END — 42 miles

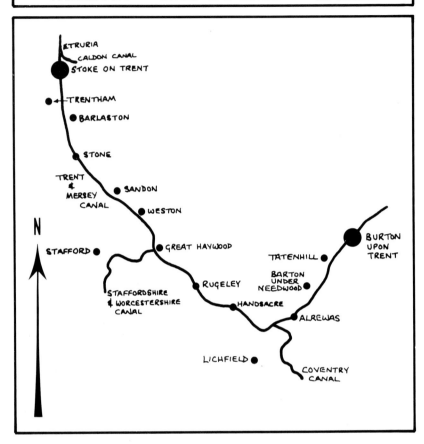

ETRURIA
CALDON CANAL
STOKE ON TRENT

←TRENTHAM

● BARLASTON

● STONE

TRENT
&
MERSEY
CANAL

● SANDON

● WESTON

N

STAFFORD ●

● GREAT HAYWOOD

STAFFORDSHIRE
& WORCESTERSHIRE
CANAL

● RUGELEY

● HANDSACRE

TATENHILL ●

BARTON
UNDER
NEEDWOOD ●

BURTON
UPON
TRENT

ALREWAS

LICHFIELD ●

COVENTRY
CANAL

TRENT & MERSEY CANAL NEAR COLWICH

TRENT & MERSEY CANAL — WALK NO 24

- 42 miles — allow 2 or more days.

ROUTE — The Trent & Mersey Canal from Burton Upon Trent to Stoke on Trent.

MAPS — O.S. 1:50,000 Landranger Series Sheet Nos -
128 — Derby & Burton Upon Trent area.
127 — Stafford, Telford & surrounding area.
118 — Stoke on Trent & Macclesfield area.

ABOUT THE WALK — I include this walk as simply the grandslam of the area covered by this book, simply as an end-to-end walk along the canal. You can do it over a weekend or longer. or over several outings. It would make a very enjoyable 3 day walk with overnight halts at —
Burton Upon Trent to Rugeley — 18 miles.
Rugeley to Stone — 12 miles.
Stone to Etruria — 12 miles.
I throw this idea out as a suggestion for your canal exploration in Staffordshire. I shall be dealing separately with the whole of the Trent & Mersey as an end-to-end walk of 92 miles in Vol 7 of this canal series!

BISHTON HALL AND TRENT & MERSEY CANAL

TAMWORTH CASTLE

TAMWORTH MARINA

THE COVENTRY CANAL

Authorised in 1768 but not fully completed until 1790.

Length — 38 miles from Fradley Junction (Trent & Mersey Canal) to Coventry. 13 locks.

The canal was engineered by James Brindley but took a long time to construct, mostly due to the fact that the original estimate of £50,000 was only sufficient to complete half the route to Atherstone. James Brindley was sacked. Ten years were to elapse before work continued on the remaining section to Fazeley in 1790. During the time lapse the Birmingham and Fazeley Canal was being made along the line of the Coventry Canal to Whittington Brook. The Coventry Canal Company later bought this section and accounts for the two names of the canal.

The aim of the canal, apart from linking into the Trent & Mersey Canal, was primarily to form cheap transport for the rich coalfields in the area. This helped to make the canal very profitable. Especially after 1790 when the Oxford Canal was completed, providing a direct link via the Thames to London. The canal continued to be prosperous long after the railways had taken over, and was still paying dividends in 1947.

THE WYRLEY AND ESSINGTON CANAL.

At Huddlesford is the junction with the Wyrley and Essington Canal which opened in 1797. The canal joined the Coventry Canal with the Birmingham Canal. It was primarily used for the transportation of coal. Today parts of it are totally lost, while the section near Lichfield although filled in can still be traced, as the walk from Huddlesford illustrates.

FAZELEY JUNCTION

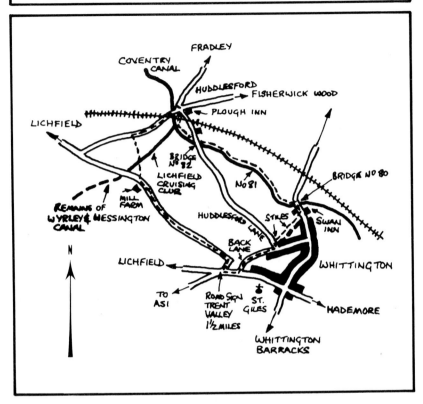

COVENTRY CANAL NEAR HUDDLESFORD

COVENTRY CANAL — WALK NO 1

3 miles — allow 1¼ hours

ROUTE — Huddlesford Bridge/Plough Inn — Coventry Canal — Swan Inn — Whittington — Mill Farm — Wyrley & Essington Canal — Huddlesford Bridge.

MAP — O.S. 1:25,000 Pathfinder Series — Sheet No SK 00/10 — Lichfield and Brownhills.

CAR PARK — No official one but roadside parking at Huddlesford Bridge.

ABOUT THE WALK — A short walk along the Coventry canal — 'between pubs' — to have a look at the Huddlesford Junction and remains of the Wyrley & Essington Canal.

WALKING INSTRUCTIONS — From Huddlesford Bridge (No 83) gain the canal towpath and walk under the bridge, keeping the canal on your right. Having passed under the railway bridge you approach the Huddlesford Junction, with the Wyre & Essington Canal, on your right. The remains of the canal at this point are used by the Lichfield Cruising Club and no right of way exists here. Continue beside the Coventry Canal past Bowman's Bridge (No 82) and in ¾ mile reach Bridge No 80 and the Swan Inn. Leave the canal here and turn right over the bridge; almost opposite the Swan Inn turn right and between houses 5 and 7 is the footpath. At the end turn right to the end of the road, where on your left is the fenced path leading to a stile. Over this keep to the field's lefthand edge with the houses also on your left. In ¼ mile reach a stile and path sign close to Highfields House and gain Huddlesfield Lane.

Turn left and a few yards later at the cross roads turn right along Back Lane. At the end of the road turn right and right again at the first road on your right signposted — Trent Valley 1½ miles. After a few yards the road turns sharp left and keep on this road for ¾ mile to Mill Farm. You ascend gently before descending to the farm entrance. On the right is a solitary house and on its lefthand side is a gate entrance. Leave the road here and cross the field to the canal bridge over the Wyrley & Essington Canal. If you continue up the road a short distance you can see on your left a stretch of the Wyrley & Essington Canal. Cross the canal bridge and keep to the righthand edge of the field to the minor road. Turn right and in just over ¼ mile you are back at Huddlesford Bridge and the Plough Inn.

LICHFIELD — dominated by its superb cathedral, whose three spires are known as "the ladies of the vale", it is well worth exploring. St Mary's Church in the Market Square has plaques to several martyrs and was the last place where anyone was burnt to death in the 17th Century. Close by is the birthplace of Dr. Samuel Johnson, now a museum.

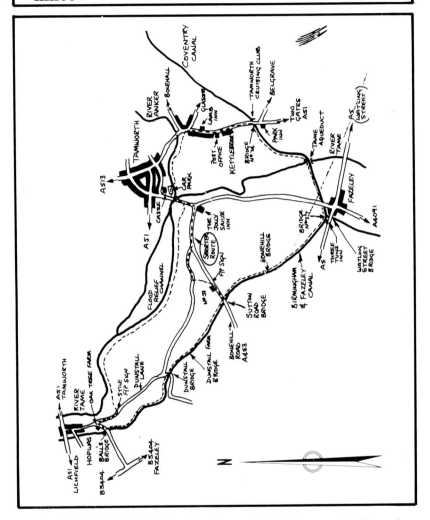

SHORTER 4½ MILE WALK — From Sutton Road Bridge ascend to the road — Bonehill Road — and turn right. Just before the Tamworth limit sign, in less than 1/4 mile, turn left onto the track and signposted footpath beside house No 51. At the end of the track turn right onto Dunstall Lane. Follow this to the new road. Cross over onto the No Through Road, following the signpost — The Jolly Sailor Inn. Turn left and cross Lady Bridge to regain the car park on your right.

TAMWORTH — a strategically important place to the Saxons and Normans. The castle, which is reputed to be haunted, is one of the few complete motte and bailey castles in England. Worth visiting is the collegiate church dedicated to St. Editha. Outside the Town Hall is a monument to Sir Ropert Peel, Prime Minister between 1842-7.

COVENTRY CANAL — WALKS 2 AND 3

- 4½ miles and 8 miles — allow 2 and 3 hours.

ROUTE — Tamworth — Bole Bridge — Kettlebrook — Coventry Canal — Fazeley Junction — Birmingham & Fazeley Canal — Ball's Bridge — Hopwas — Flood Relief Channel — River Tame — Lady Bridge — Tamworth

MAPS — O.S. 1:25,000 Pathfinder Series Sheet Nos SK 20/30 — Tamworth and Sheet No SK 00/10 — Lichfield and Brownhills.

CAR PARK — beneath Tamworth Castle, close to River Tame and Lady Bridge.

ABOUT THE WALKS — From beneath the impressive castle you cross the park to Kettleworth to gain the Coventry Canal. You follow this across the River Tame to the major canal junction at Fazeley. Here you pick up the Birmingham & Fazeley Canal section of the Coventry Canal and follow it to Hopwas, where there are two inns. You return close to the flood relief channel to Lady Bridge. The shorter walk leaves the Birmingham & Fazeley Canal after 1¼ miles at Sutton Road Bridge, and via paths and roads goes directly to the Lady Bridge and the Jolly Sailor Inn.

WALKING INSTRUCTIONS — Walk through the car park and cross the footbridge over the River Anker. Turn left and keep the river on your left before bearing right and passing under two bridges, aiming for the righthand side of the multi-arched railway bridge — Bole Bridge. At the roundabout in front of it turn right onto the minor road to Kettlebrook — Kettlebrook Road. Pass the Lamb Inn and in 1/2 mile reach the canal bridge — No 74 — over the Coventry Canal. On your left is the Tamworth Cruising Club and just ahead is the Park Inn. Turn right down to the towpath and keep the canal on your left as you follow the path. In 1/2 mile cross the small aqueduct over the River Tame and in a further 1/2 mile reach Fazeley Junction. On your left is Watling Street Bridge and the Three Tuns Inn.

Keep the canal on your left as you now follow the Birmingham & Fazeley Canal. After 3/4 mile pass under Bonehill Bridge and in a further 1/2 mile reach Sutton Road Bridge; here the shorter route leads directly for Lady Bridge. Continue beside the canal for almost 2 miles to Ball's Bridge on the outskirts of Hopwas. If you continue you will reach two canalside inns — the Chequers Inn and the Red Lion. From Ball's Bridge gain the road and turn right along it past Oak Tree Farm. Just afterwards turn right along Dunstall Lane, and in 1/4 mile at the stile and footpath sign turn left and soon approach the banks of the flood relief channel. The right of way on the map shows the route is further inland, but on the ground all the stiles and footpath arrows are close to the channel. It is these you should use. You keep beside the channel for the next 1½ miles with Tamworth Castle increasing in size. As you near Lady Bridge you bear right to a footpath bridge and follow the defined path to a kissing gate. Turn left and cross Lady Bridge and turn right into the car park.

STOURPORT

STOURPORT — JUNCTION WITH RIVER SEVERN

THE STAFFORDSHIRE & WORCESTER-SHIRE CANAL

Engineered by James Brindley and opened in 1772, having cost more than £100,000.

Length — 46 miles from Great Haywood junction on the Trent & Mersey Canal to Stourport on the River Severn. 43 locks.

The Staffs & Worcs Canal, as it is affectionately called, joined the Rivers Severn, Mersey and Trent together and was immediately profitable. The canal faced competition with the building of the Worcester & Birmingham Canal in 1815 and in 1835 part of the Birmingham & Liverpool Canal. Both provided more direct routes. Like all canals, the coming of the railways dealt it a severe blow in the 1860s but by early this century was little used. Today it is primarily a pleasure craft route and, as can be seen from the walks described, is a particularly attractive canal through very pleasant scenery. The Stourport Basin and junction with the River Severn is breathtakingly beautiful.

MILFORD CROSSOVER BRIDGE — STAFFORDSHIRE & WORCES-TERSHIRE CANAL

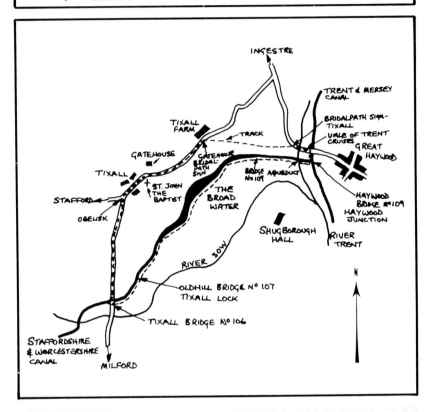

TIXALL GATE HOUSE

TIXALL — the Elizabethan gate house built in 1575 is all that remains of Tixall Hall, home of the Aston family. Mary Queen of Scots was held captive in the Hall for two weeks in August 1586. She was also imprisoned in Tutbury Castle and Chartley Castle.

STAFFORDSHIRE & WORCESTERSHIRE CANAL — WALK NO 1

4 miles — allow 2 hours.

ROUTE — Tixall Bridge — Staffordshire & Worcestershire Canal — Haywood Junction — Haywood Mill — Tixall Farm — Tixall — Tixall Bridge.

MAP — O.S. 1:25,000 Pathfinder Series Sheet No SJ 82/92 — Stafford.

CAR PARK — No official one. ½ mile to the south is a carpark on Milford Common.

ABOUT THE WALK — A short walk along the canal to its junction with the Trent & Mersey Canal, near Great Haywood. From here you cross fields to the impressive Tixall village and see at close hand the magnificent Elizabethan gate-house of the former hall. A short road walk returns you to Tixall Bridge where you began.

WALKING INSTRUCTIONS — From Tixall Bridge (No 106) descend to the canal and turn right under the bridge, heading eastwards. Keep the canal on your lefthand side and in little more than ¼ mile reach Tixall Lock. Continue beside the canal, past Broad Water and on to Haywood Junction and Haywood Bridge No 109. Turn right and cross the bridge to briefly walk beside the Trent & Mersey Canal. Almost immediately ascend to the road bridge — Great Haywood is on your right with the Fox and Hounds Inn ¼ mile away! Turn left over the bridge, past the Vale of Trent Cruises, and just past the last house on your left is a gate and bridlepath sign — Tixall. Turn left through the gate and keep on the defined gated track for ½ mile to the minor road in front of Tixall Farm. You gain the road close to a circular gatehouse and bridlepath sign. Turn left along the road with views of the Elizabethan four storey high gate house. Pass the church dedicated to St. John the Baptist on your left, and ¼ mile later at the road junction, the obelisk. Turn left on the Milford Road and in ¾ mile regain Tixall Bridge where you began.

NARROW BOATS AT HAYWOOD JUNCTION

WALK 2 — TIXALL BRIDGE — STAFFORD — 5 miles

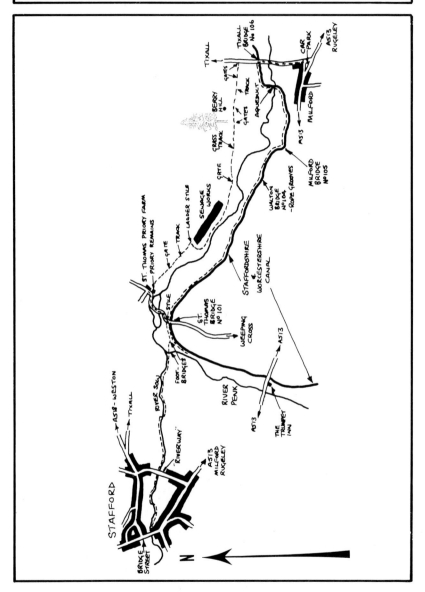

STAFFORD — well worth exploring if time permits, with many notable buildings. Of particular note is the Ancient High House in Greengate Street, in the central shopping area and now a Visitor's Centre and Information Centre. It is the largest timber framed building in England and was built in 1595. The orginal town was on an ancient track-way on an island in the middle of marshland. The town's name is Saxon in origin and means a ford at a landing place — STAITH-FORD.

STAFFORDSHIRE & WORCESTRSHIRE CANAL — WALK NO 2

5 miles — allow 2 hours. The extension to Stafford is 1½ miles one way.

ROUTE — Tixall Bridge — Staffordshire & Worcestershire Canal to St. Thomas's bridge No 101 — St Thomas Priory Farm — River Sow — Berry Hill — Tixall Bridge.

EXTENSION — River Sow from Stafford to St Thomas bridge No 101.

MAP — O.S. 1:25,000 Pathfinder Series Sheet No SJ 82/92 — Stafford.

CAR PARK — No official one. Car Park ½ due south of Tixall Bridge on Milford Common, beside Cannock Chase. If starting from Stafford many car parks in central area, near Bridge Street.

ABOUT THE WALK — A fascinating walk along the canal in surprisingly quiet surroundings. You return over the fields passing the remains of St Thomas Priory before walking close to the River Sow to gain a track through woodland back to Tixall Bridge. The path is little used and does not correspond to what is shown on the O.S. map, as you would walk through a sewage works! But despite this it is an enjoyable walk and full of impressive canal features. The walk can be started from Bridge Street in Stafford with a defined path along the banks of the River Sow to St Thomas Bridge. Close by the canal turns sharp left and heads southwards to Penkridge and Kinver; an area to be explored in a future volume!

WALKING INSTRUCTIONS — From Tixall Bridge (No 106) descend to the towpath and turn left along it (westwards) with the canal on your right. In just over ¼ mile cross the River Sow aqueduct and in a further ½ mile reach Bridge No 105 — Milford Bridge — and a crossover one. Cross over and now keep the canal on your lefthand side. The next bridge has some excellent rope grooves. You keep beside the canal for a further 1½ miles to St Thomas Bridge — No 101. Hear you leave the canal, but it is worth continuing a little way to see the remains of a lock which served as the start of a mile long branch, using the River Sow, to Stafford. Gain the road and head (right) northwards and in a few yards on your left is a stile and the path which leads to a footbridge over the River Penk close to its junction with the River Sow, which you can walk beside to Bridge Street in Stafford.

Continue along the road over the River Sow Bridge to St Thomas Priory Farm on your right. Almost opposite a side road on your left turn right through the farm and approaching the main building bear left on a track to a gate. Keep on this gated track past a small rocky outcrop on your left and on towards the sewage works. Just before the tarmaced road to it on your right is a ladder stile. Ascend this and descend the field close to the perimeter fence on your left to reach the River Sow. Keep it on your right and in just over ½ mile cross a footbridge. The last time I was here I saw a flock of Canada Geese on the other bank! Continue close to the river for another ¼ mile to where the river and field boundary on your left almost meet. Here is a gate and go through this and bear right through marshy ground to reach a gate well above the woodland on your right. Through the gate you soon pick up a defined track which leads to the base of the pine-covered Berry Hill. The track is well gated as you continue ahead on it all the way to the minor road near Tixall Bridge ½ mile away. Turn right at the road and in ¼ mile regain Tixall Bridge and the canal.

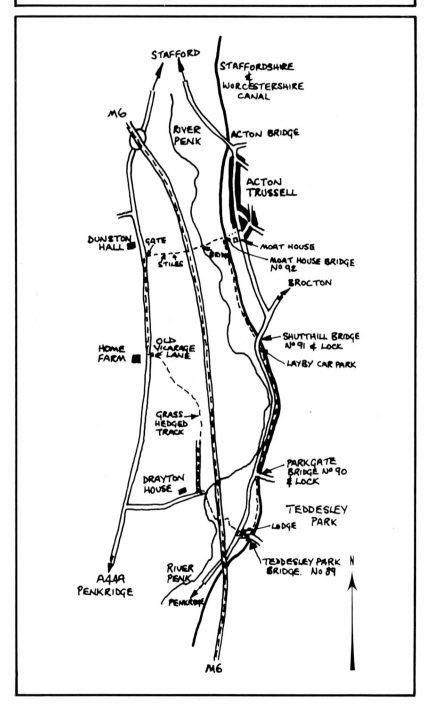

STAFFORDSHIRE & WORCESTERSHIRE CANAL — WALK NO 3

- 4 miles — allow 1½ hours.

ROUTE — Shutthill Bridge (No 91) — Staffs & Worcs Canal — Teddesley Park Bridge (No 89) — Lower Drayton — Home Farm — Dunston — Acton Trussell — Shutthill Bridge.

MAP — O.S. 1:25,000 Pathfinder Series Sheet No SJ 81/91 — Cannock (North).

CAR PARK — Lay-bys beside the canal at Shutthill Bridge, 1/2 mile south of Acton Trussell.

ABOUT THE WALK — Although the area is dominated by the M6, the canal makes a peaceful haven and is full of interest with locks, marina and impressive buildings. The village of Acton Trussell is close by and is worth exploring if time permits. This is one of the rare walks where there is no inn on the way — sorry!

WALKING INSTRUCTIONS — From the lay-by at Shutthill Bridge gain the canal and turn right along the towpath, keeping the canal on your lefthand side. For the next 1/2 mile the minor road parallels the canal to Parkgate Bridge No 90. Just after the bridge is Parkgate Lock and Midland Chandlers on your left. Continue beside the canal for a further 1/4 mile to the next bridge — Teddesley Park Bridge No 89. After passing under it turn right, leaving the canal, and gain the track and turn left along it past the lodge on your right to the minor road. Turn right and almost immediately left at the gate by the footpath sign. Cross the short field to the kissing gate and tunnel beneath the M6. Walk through to the next kissing gate and bear right across the field to the small bridge over the River Penk, and footpath sign — Teddesley Park. Upon reaching the minor road turn right along it, and in 1/4 mile keep ahead onto a grass track. After 1/2 mile along here you walk along Old Vicarage Lane to the A449 road, opposite Home Farm.

Turn right along the tarmaced path close to the road and in 1/4 mile pass a lay-by. A little further on your left is the drive to Dunston Hall — North Staffordshire Polytechnic. A few yards later on your right and below the path in the hedge is a small wooden gate. Turn right here and descend the field to a wooden stile. This is followed by another one as you head for another tunnel beneath the M6. On the other side continue to a footbridge over the River Penk and in another 150 yards reach the canal. Here turn right and follow the towpath and in 1/2 mile regain Shutthill Bridge. Before walking along the towpath, if you cross the bridge you can enter the village of Acton Trussell with its attractive moated house, now a restaurant.

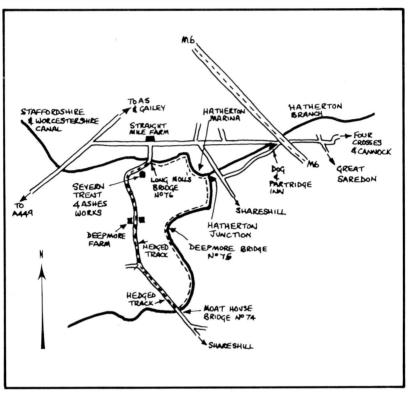

ACTON MOAT BRIDGE — No 92

STAFFORDSHIRE & WORCESTERSHIRE CANAL — WALK NO 4

3½ miles — allow 1½ hours.

ROUTE — Long Moll's Bridge — Hatherton Junction — Staffs & Worcs Canal — Moat House Bridge — Deepmore Bridge.

MAP — O.S. 1:25,000 Pathfinder Series Sheet No SJ 80/90 — Wolverhampton (North).

CAR PARK — No official one.

ABOUT THE WALK — a short walk in the southern end of the county, basically to explore the junction with the Hatherton Branch. Parts of this can be walked towards Cannock. For me I had to end my explorations here for this book, as two future volume will deal with the Hatherton Branch more fully together with the Birmingham Canals. It is a very pleasant walk in remote country. The nearest inn is the Dog and Partridge 1/2 mile along the Hatherton Branch, but it can only be reached by road as there is no towpath.

WALKING INSTRUCTIONS — Starting from Long Moll's Bridge (No 76) just down the road from Straight Mile Farm, descend to the towpath and turn right along it keeping the canal on your lefthand side. In a 1/3 mile reach Hatherton Marina on your left and shortly afterwards the junction with the Hatherton Branch. Continue along the canal, passing a moated area on the other side of the canal on your left. 1/4 mile later pass under Deepmore Bridge, No 76, and in a further 1/2 mile Moat House Bridge, No 74. Here, after passing under the bridge, ascend the steps and gain the hedged road/track. Turn left along it, and in a 1/3 mile at a junction of tracks keep right on the hedged track and descend gently to Deepmore Farm. Here the track becomes a tarmaced road as you continue ahead and in 1/2 mile regain Long Moll's Bridge.

HATHERTON JUNCTION

73

WALK 5 — END TO END — 15 miles

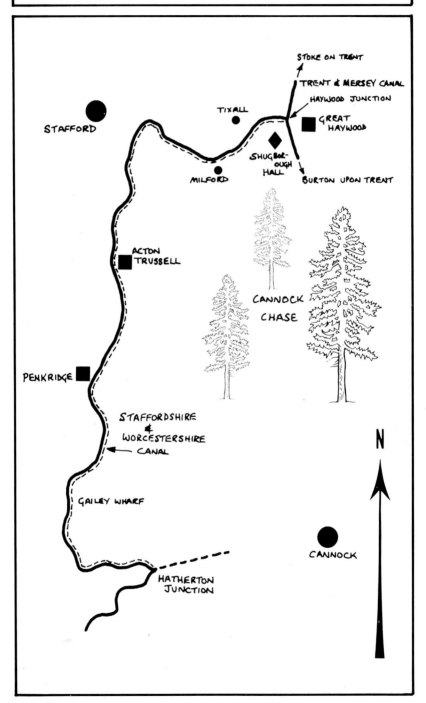

STAFFORDSHIRE & WORCESTERSHIRE CANAL — WALK NO 5

15 miles — allow 6 hours.

ROUTE — Hatherton Junction — Staffs & Worcs Canal to Haywood Junction (Trent & Mersey Canal).

MAPS — O.S. 1;25,000 Pathfinder Series Sheet Nos SJ 80/90 — Wolverhampton (North); SJ 81/91 — Cannock (North); and SJ 82/92 — Stafford.

ABOUT THE WALK & WALKING INSTRUCTIONS — I have included this more as a suggestion for a longer walk following the canal "end to end". Having walked it all in stages I felt it made a very enjoyable walk especially in the southern half around Penkridge. This village is particularly interesting and worth leaving the canal to explore more fully. The whole walk follows the canal to Haywood Junction — the Trent & Mersey Canal — and passes through some delightful sections of peaceful canal walking. Passing close to central Stafford you can also deviate here or even end here, making a walk of about 10 miles from Hatherton Junction.

PENKRIDGE — Contains several timber framed buildings including the White Hart Inn. The church dates from the 14th Century and contains several interesting monuments and features.

NARROW BOAT ON STAFFS & WORCS CANAL Nr PARKGATE LOCK

ABOUT THE WALKS —

Whilst every care is taken detailing and describing the walks in this book, it should be borne in mind that the countryside changes by the seasons and the work of man. I have described the walks to the best of my ability, detailing what I have found on the walk in the way of stiles and signs. Obviously with the passage of time stiles become broken or replaced by a ladder stile or even a small gate. Signs too have a habit of being broken or pushed over. All the routes follow rights of way and only on rare occasions will you have to overcome obstacles in its path, such as a barbed wire fence or electric fence.

The seasons bring occasional problems whilst out walking which should also be bourne in mind. In the height of summer paths become overgrown and you will have to fight your way through in a few places. In low lying areas the fields are full of crops, and although the pathline goes straight across it may be more practical to walk round the field edge to get to the next stile or gate. In summer the ground is generally dry but in autumn and winter, especially because of our climate, the surface can be decidedly wet and slippery; sometimes even glutonous mud!

These comments are part of countryside walking which help to make your walk more interesting or briefly frustrating. Standing in a farmyard up to your ankles in mud might not be funny at the time but upon reflection was one of the highlights of the walk!

OLDHILL BRIDGE, STAFFORDSHIRE & WORCESTERSHIRE CANAL

CANAL FEATURES — to look for

STOP PLANKS — in various places can be seen vertical grooves in the canal walls — especially near bridges — with handled planks stacked nearby. The planks are slotted into the grooves sealing the canal while repairs or cleaning of the drained section is carried out.

ROPE GROOVES — on the side of bridges, sometimes with either cast iron or wooden shields, can be seen the grooves cut by the horse tow lines over the decades, such as the photograph below at the junction of the Trent & Mersey Canal with the Staffordshire & Worcestershire Canal.

TURNOVER/CROSSOVER BRIDGES — in a few places the towpath switches sides of the canal and a bridge was built to enable the horse to cross over without unhitching the line. The Trent & Mersey Canal has several and on the Staffordshire & Worcestershire Canal — Milford Bridge No 105 is a particularly fine example.

SWING BRIDGES — as the name implies, the bridge could be swung out of the way to allow boats to pass.

BALANCED BRIDGES — bridges finely balanced that can be either pushed upwards out of the way or lowered across the canal.

SKEW BRIDGES — most canal bridges are built at right angles to the canal. In a few cases to avoid the Z bend in the road the bridge was built at an angle.

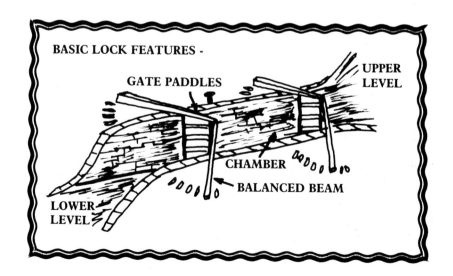

BASIC LOCK FEATURES -

GATE PADDLES

UPPER LEVEL

CHAMBER

BALANCED BEAM

LOWER LEVEL

CANAL MUSEUMS

1. The National Waterways Museum,
The Boat Museum,
Dockyard Road,
Ellesmere Port,
South Wirral.
L65 4EF Tel. No 051-355 5017

2. The National Waterways Museum,
Llanthony Warehouse,
Gloucester Docks,
Gloucester.
GL1 2EH Tel No. 0452 — 25524

3. British Waterways Board,
Waterways Museum,
Stoke Bruerne,
Towcester,
Northants.

NATIONAL BOAT MUSEUM, ELLESMERE PORT

OTHERS OF RELATED INTEREST -

1. Ancient High House,
Stafford.
Tel No. Stafford 223181

2. Bass Museum,
Burton Upon Trent.
Tel No. Burton 45301

3. Chatterley Whitfield Mining Museum,
Nr. Tunstall,
Stoke on Trent.
Tel No. S.O.T. 813337

4. City Museum & Art Gallery,
Hanley,
Stoke on Trent.
Tel No. S.O.T. 202173

5. Gladstone Pottery Museum,
Longton,
Stoke on Trent.
Tel No. S.O.T. 319232

6. Izaak Waltons Cottage,
Nr. Stafford.
Tel No. Stafford 760278

7. Shugborough Hall,
Nr. Stafford.
Tel No. Little Haywood 881388

8. Trentham Gardens,
Trentham.
Tel No. S.O.T. 657341

9. Wedgwood Visitor Centre,
Barlaston.
Tel No. S.O.T. 204218

10. Royal Doulton,
Tours and Museum,
Stoke on Trent.
Tel No. S.O.T. 85747

11. Minton,
Tours and Museum,
Stoke on Trent.
Tel No. S.O.T. 49171

BASS MUSEUM, BURTON UPON TRENT

CANAL SOCIETIES & USEFUL ADDRESSES -

British Waterways Board,
Information Centre,
Melbury House,
Melbury Terrace,
London.
NW1 6JX

Trent & Mersey Canal Society,
H.L. Potter,
350, Boldmere Road,
Sutton Coldfield,
West Midlands.
B73 5EY

Coventry Canal Society,
J. Stranger,
62, Keresley Road,
Radford,
Coventry,
Warwickshire.

Caldon Canal Society,
H. V. Turner,
Broad Street Post Office,
Hanley,
Stoke on Trent,
Staffs
ST1 4JH

Staffordshire & Worcestershire Canal Society,
c/o, Eversleigh,
Langley Road,
Lower Penn,
Wolverhampton.
West Midlands.

BRIDGE AT HAYWOOD JUNCTION

SUGGESTED FURTHER READING —
a random selection

The Canals of the East Midlands Charles Hadfield David & Charles
The Canals of the West Midlands Charles Hadfield David & Charles
British Canals — an Illustrated History Charles Hadfield David & Charles 1979
James Brindley H. Bode Shire Publictions 1973
The Trent & Mersey Canal Lindsay David & Charles 1979
Nicholson/Ordnance Survey Guide to the Waterways — Vol 2 — Central
Nicholson/Ordnance Survey Guide to the Waterways — Vol 3 — North
Cheshire Ring Canal Walk — Vols 1 to 11 — Cheshire County Council publications.
Canal Companion Cheshire Ring J.M.Pearson 1986
Discovering Canals in Britain Peter L.Smith Shire Publications 1981
Discovering Lost Canals Ronald Russell Shire Publications
Inland Waterways Guide — 1988

KING'S BROMLEY WHARF

OTHER CANAL WALK BOOKS BY JOHN N. MERRILL

Vol 1 — Derbyshire and Nottinghamshire.
- more than 30 walks on the Chesterfield, Cromford, Erewash, Nutbrook, Derby, Nottingham and Trent & Mersey Canals.

Vol 2 — Cheshire and Staffordshire.
- more than 40 walks on the Peak Forest, Macclesfield, Caldon and Trent & Mersey Canals.

FORTHCOMING -

Vol 4 — The Cheshire Ring
— walk guide in stages to the 97 mile walk around the Ring on the Macclesfield, Peak Forest, Ashton, Rochdale, Bridgewater, and Trent & Mersey Canals.

Vol 5 — Nottinghamshire, Leicestershire and Lincolnshire.
— deals with River Trent, Grantham Canal, River Soar, Witham Navigation, and Foss Dyke Navigation.

Vol 6 — South Yorkshire.
— Barnsley Canal, River Don and Navigation, Staniforth and Keadby canal.

Vol 7 — The Trent & Mersey Canal.
— walk guide to the whole 93 mile length of the canal.
To be walked in stages or as a magnificent week's walk.

Vol 8 & 9 — The Birmingham Canals.

OTHER BOOKS BY JOHN N. MERRILL PUBLISHED BY JNM PUBLICATIONS

DAY WALK GUIDES —

SHORT CIRCULAR WALKS IN THE PEAK DISTRICT
LONG CIRCULAR WALKS IN THE PEAK DISTRICT
CIRCULAR WALKS IN WESTERN PEAKLAND
SHORT CIRCULAR WALKS IN THE STAFFORDSHIRE MOORLANDS
SHORT CIRCULAR WALKS AROUND THE TOWNS AND VILLAGES OF
THE PEAK DISTRICT
SHORT CIRCULAR WALKS AROUND MATLOCK
SHORT CIRCULAR WALKS IN THE DUKERIES
SHORT CIRCULAR WALKS IN SOUTH YORKSHIRE
SHORT CIRCULAR WALKS AROUND DERBY
SHORT CIRCULAR WALKS AROUND BAKEWELL
SHORT CIRCULAR WALKS AROUND BUXTON
SHORT CIRCULAR WALKS AROUND NOTTINGHAMSHIRE
SHORT CIRCULAR WALKS ON THE NORTHERN MOORS
40 SHORT CIRCULAR PEAK DISTRICT WALKS
SHORT CIRCULAR WALKS IN THE HOPE VALLEY

INSTRUCTION & RECORD —

HIKE TO BE FIT..STROLLING WITH JOHN
THE JOHN MERRILL WALK RECORD BOOK

CANAL WALK GUIDES —

VOL ONE — DERBYSHIRE AND NOTTINGHAMSHIRE
VOL TWO — CHESHIRE AND STAFFORDSHIRE
VOL THREE — STAFFORDSHIRE
VOL FOUR — THE CHESHIRE RING
VOL FIVE — LINCOLNSHIRE & NOTTINGHAMSHIRE
VOL SIX — SOUTH YORKSHIRE
VOL SEVEN — THE TRENT & MERSEY CANAL

DAY CHALLENGE WALKS —

JOHN MERRILL'S PEAK DISTRICT CHALLENGE WALK
JOHN MERRILL'S YORKSHIRE DALES CHALLENGE WALK
JOHN MERRILL'S NORTH YORKSHIRE MOORS CHALLENGE WALK
PEAK DISTRICT END TO END WALKS
THE LITTLE JOHN CHALLENGE WALK
JOHN MERRILL'S LAKELAND CHALLENGE WALK
JOHN MERRILL'S STAFFORDSHIRE MOORLAND CHALLENGE WALK
JOHN MERRILL'S DARK PEAK CHALLENGE WALK

MULTIPLE DAY WALKS —

THE RIVERS' WAY
PEAK DISTRICT HIGH LEVEL ROUTE
PEAK DISTRICT MARATHONS
THE LIMEY WAY
THE PEAKLAND WAY

COAST WALKS —

ISLE OF WIGHT COAST WALK
PEMBROKESHIRE COAST PATH
THE CLEVELAND WAY

HISTORICAL GUIDES —

DERBYSHIRE INNS
HALLS AND CASTLES OF THE PEAK DISTRICT & DERBYSHIRE
TOURING THE PEAK DISTRICT AND DERBYSHIRE BY CAR
DERBYSHIRE FOLKLORE
LOST INDUSTRIES OF DERBYSHIRE
PUNISHMENT IN DERBYSHIRE
CUSTOMS OF THE PEAK DISTRICT AND DERBYSHIRE
WINSTER — A VISITOR'S GUIDE
ARKWRIGHT OF CROMFORD
TALES FROM THE MINES by GEOFFREY CARR
PEAK DISTRICT PLACE NAMES by MARTIN SPRAY

JOHN'S MARATHON WALKS —

TURN RIGHT AT LAND'S END
WITH MUSTARD ON MY BACK
TURN RIGHT AT DEATH VALLEY
EMERALD COAST WALK

COLOUR GUIDES —

THE PEAK DISTRICT. . . Something to remember her by.

SKETCH BOOKS — by John Creber

NORTH STAFFORDSHIRE SKETCHBOOK

CALENDARS

1989 JOHN MERRILL PEAK DISTRICT WALK A MONTH CALENDAR

WALK RECORD CHART

Date Walked

TRENT & MERSEY CANAL

WALK 1 — WILLINGTON — 2½ miles (2 walks) ....

WALK 2 — STRETTON — 3 miles ....

WALK 3 — STRETTON — 2½ miles ....

WALK 4 — BURTON UPON TRENT — 4½ miles ....

WALK 5 — BRANSTON — 6 miles ....

WALK 6 — BARTON TURN — 5 miles ....

WALK 7 — ALREWAS — 6 miles ....

WALK 8 — FRADLEY JUNCTION — 5 miles ... *16/4/90* ....

WALK 9 — HANDSACRE — 4½ miles ....

WALK 10 — HANDSACRE — 4 miles ....

WALK 11 — RUGELEY — 5½ miles ....

WALK 12 — RUGELEY — 3 miles ...... *23/4/90* ....

WALK 13 — LITTLE HAYWOOD — 4 miles ....

WALK 14 — SEVEN SPRINGS — 7 miles ....

WALK 15 — GREAT HAYWOOD — 5 miles ....

WALKS 16 & 17 — WESTON — 4 & 7 miles ....

WALK 18 — ASTON — 4 miles .... *29/2/90* ....

WALK 19 — WESTON — 7 miles ....

WALK 20 — STONE — 5 miles ....

WALK 21 — MEAFORD — 7 miles ....

WALK 22 — BARLASTON — 3½ miles ....

WALK 23 — BARLASTON — 5 miles ....

WALK 24 — END TO END — 42 miles ....

COVENTRY CANAL

WALK 1 — HUDDLESFORD — 3 miles ....

WALKS 2 & 3 — TAMWORTH — 4½ and 8 miles ....

STAFFORDSHIRE & WORCESTERSHIRE CANAL

WALK 1 — TIXALL BRIDGE — TIXALL — 4 miles ....

WALK 2 — TIXALL BRIDGE — STAFFORD — 5 miles ....

WALK 3 — ACTON TRUSSELL — 4 miles ....

WALK 4 — HATHERTON JUNCTION — 3½ miles ....

WALK 5 — END TO END — 15 miles ....

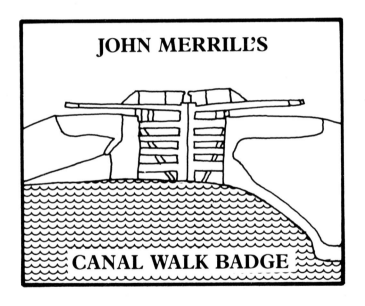

JOHN MERRILL'S CANAL WALK BADGE

Walk six or more of the walks in this book and send details to John N. Merrill at JNM PUBLICATIONS, enclosing £2.00 for a special four colour embroidered badge.

EQUIPMENT NOTES — some personal thoughts

BOOTS — preferably with a full leather upper, of medium weight, with a vibram sole. I always add a foam cushioned insole to help cushion the base of my feet.

SOCKS — I generally wear two thick pairs as this helps minimise blisters. The inner pair are of loop stitch variety and approximately 80% wool. The outer are a thick rib pair of approximately 80% wool.

WATERPROOFS — for general walking I wear a T shirt or shirt with a cotton wind jacket on top. You generate heat as you walk and I prefer to layer my clothes to avoid getting too hot. Depending on the season will dictate how many layers you wear. In soft rain I just use my wind jacket for I know it quickly dries out. In heavy downpours I slip on a neoprene lined cagoule, and although hot and clammy it does keep me reasonably dry. Only in extreme conditions will I don overtrousers, much preferring to get wet and feel comfortable.

FOOD — as I walk I carry bars of chocolate, for they provide instant energy and are light to carry. In winter a flask of hot coffee is welcome. I never carry water and find no hardship from doing so, but this is a personal matter! From experience I find the more I drink the more I want and sweat. You should always carry some extra food such as Kendal mint cake, for emergencies.

RUCKSACKS — for day walking I use a climbing rucksac of about 40 litre capacity and although it leaves excess space it does mean that the sac is well padded, with an internal frame and padded shoulder straps. Inside apart from the basics for the day I carry gloves, balaclava, spare pullover and a pair of socks.

MAP & COMPASS — when I am walking I always have the relevant map — preferably the 1:25,000 scale — open in my hand. This enables me to constantly check that I am walking the right way. In case of bad weather I carry a compass, which once mastered gives you complete confidence in thick cloud or mist.

MILFORD BRIDGE — STAFFORDSHIRE & WORCESTERSHIRE CANAL

87

REMEMBER AND OBSERVE THE COUNTRY CODE

Enjoy the countryside and respect its life and work.

Guard against all risk of fire.

Fasten all gates.

Keep your dogs under close control.

Keep to public paths across farmland.

Use gates and stiles to cross fences, hedges and walls.

Leave livestock, crops and machinery alone.

Take your litter home — pack it in, pack it out.

Help to keep all water clean.

Protect wildlife, plants and trees.

Take special care on country roads.

Make no unnecessary noise.

STAFFORDSHIRE & WORCESTERSHIRE CANAL — AQUEDUCT OVER RIVER PENK

THE HIKER'S CODE

* Hike only along marked routes — do not leave the trail.

* Use stiles to climb fences; close gates.

* Camp only in designated campsites.

* Carry a light-weight stove.

* Leave the Trail cleaner than you found it.

* Leave flowers and plants for others to enjoy.

* Keep dogs on a leash.

* Protect and do not disturb wildlife.

* Use the trail at your own risk.

* Leave only your thanks — take nothing but photographs.

COLWICH LOCK

HAYWOOD JUNCTION SIGN

ROPE GROOVES AT HAYWOOD JUNCTION

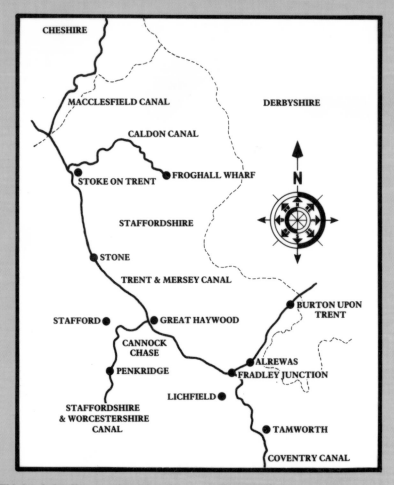

This book details more than 30 walks on the Trent & Mersey, Staffordshire & Worcestershire, and Coventry Canals in Staffordshire. Each walk is illustrated by photographs and a map and each makes an excellent walk for all the family as you explore the transport system of two centuries ago. All are circular and include both long and short walks with numerous pubs along the way.

Cover photograph — Tatenhill Lock, Trent & Mersey Canal, Nr Branston. — by John N. Merrill

a J.N.M. PUBLICATION

£4.95

ISBN 0-907496-62-8

9 780907 496625